Cambridge Elements ≡

Elements in Publishing and Book Culture
edited by
Samantha Rayner
University College London
Leah Tether
University of Bristol

PUBLISHING IN A MEDIEVAL MONASTERY

The View from Twelfth-Century Engelberg

Benjamin Pohl
University of Bristol

CAMBRIDGE
UNIVERSITY PRESS

CAMBRIDGE
UNIVERSITY PRESS

Shaftesbury Road, Cambridge CB2 8EA, United Kingdom

One Liberty Plaza, 20th Floor, New York, NY 10006, USA

477 Williamstown Road, Port Melbourne, VIC 3207, Australia

314–321, 3rd Floor, Plot 3, Splendor Forum, Jasola District Centre,
New Delhi – 110025, India

103 Penang Road, #05–06/07, Visioncrest Commercial, Singapore 238467

Cambridge University Press is part of Cambridge University Press & Assessment,
a department of the University of Cambridge.

We share the University's mission to contribute to society through the pursuit of
education, learning and research at the highest international levels of excellence.

www.cambridge.org
Information on this title: www.cambridge.org/9781009202558

DOI: 10.1017/9781009202541

First published 2023

A catalogue record for this publication is available from the British Library.

ISBN 978-1-009-20255-8 Paperback
ISSN 2514-8524 (online)
ISSN 2514-8516 (print)

Publishing in a Medieval Monastery

The View from Twelfth-Century Engelberg

Elements in Publishing and Book Culture

DOI: 10.1017/9781009202541

First published online: July 2023

Benjamin Pohl

University of Bristol

Author for correspondence: Benjamin Pohl, benjamin.pohl@bristol.ac.uk

ABSTRACT: This Element contributes to the burgeoning field of medieval publishing studies with a case study of the books produced at the Benedictine monastery of Engelberg under its celebrated twelfth-century abbot, Frowin (1143–78). Frowin was the first abbot of Engelberg whose book provision policy relied on domestic production serviced by an internal scribal workforce, and his tenure marked the first major expansion of the community's library. This Element's in-depth discussion of nearly forty colophons inscribed in the books made for this library during Frowin's transformative abbacy offers a fresh perspective on monastic publishing practice in the twelfth century by directing our view to a mode of publication that has received only limited attention in scholarship to date.

KEYWORDS: publishing, monasticism, Middle Ages, manuscripts, abbots

ISBNs: 9781009202558 (PB), 9781009202541 (OC)

ISSNs: 2514-8524 (online), 2514-8516 (print)

Contents

1 Introduction: Publishing in Medieval Monasteries

In his recent trade book *The Posthumous Papers of the Manuscripts Club* (2022), Christopher de Hamel refers to medieval monasteries as 'the earliest publishing houses, making books and distributing them to other abbeys and communities, who, in turn, transcribed texts and passed them on', when '[t]here was no method of professional publication'.[1] This highly evocative notion of medieval publishing – and specifically medieval monastic publishing – communicated confidently to the book's readership is one familiar to scholars, though within the academy, the use of terms such as *publishing* and/or *publication* prior to the age of print remains subject to scepticism and, as Felicity Riddy noted some twenty years ago, 'nervous inverted commas are a hallmark of the subject'.[2] This is not the place to revive this debate.[3] Suffice to say that the *communis opinio* emerging in the field and adopted in this Element is that '*publishing* as a term is applicable to manuscript cultures' such as those that governed the transmission and dissemination of knowledge in twelfth-century Europe.[4]

---

[1] C. de Hamel, *The Posthumous Papers of the Manuscripts Club* (London: Allen Lane, 2022), pp. 11 and 36.

[2] F. Riddy, '"Publication" before Print: The Case of Julian of Norwich', in J. Crick and A. Walsham (eds.), *The Uses of Script and Print, 1300–1700* (Cambridge: Cambridge University Press, 2003), pp. 29–49 (p. 30).

[3] For a good (and relatively recent) overview, I refer the reader to L. Tether, *Publishing the Grail in Medieval and Renaissance France* (Cambridge: D. S. Brewer, 2017), pp. 13–26. Also compare the polemic think pieces in preparation for the *Gazette du livre médiéval* under the auspices of David Ganz, forthcoming. Note that the etymology of the modern English verb 'to publish' – from Latin *publicus* – *publicare* ('to make public') > Old/Middle French *poeplier/publier* – *puepleié* (past participle) > Anglo-Norman *poplier/pubblier* > Middle English *publishen* – is not specific to a given medium or materiality; see 'publish, v.', *OED Online*, www.oed.com/view/Entry/154072.

[4] S. Niskanen, 'The Emergence of an Authorial Culture: Publishing in Denmark in the Long Twelfth Century', in A. C. Horn (ed.), *The Meaning of Media: Texts and Materiality in Medieval Scandinavia* (Berlin: De Gruyter, 2021), pp. 71–92 (p. 72).

Recent scholarship has produced a robust body of research dedicated to different forms and formats of publishing in the Middle Ages.[5] Most attention so far has been devoted to what Riddy, in identifying four main *modes* of publication, refers to as 'authorial publishing' – terminology that has been nuanced further by others.[6] Samu Niskanen, for instance, speaks of 'an authorial act of releasing a work to a public', in which '[t]he vehicle was a manuscript',[7] if not always or necessarily an autograph. Authorial publication and the various processes and agents involved in it continue to form the dominant focus of premodern publishing studies dedicated to manuscript culture(s). And yet, as Ian Doyle observes in his study of publication by medieval religious orders, authorship – and, by extension, authorial release – constitutes but '*one* of the processes involved in the publication and production of books', which 'in any era … will consist of, on one hand, a range of recent compositions and compilations or fresh versions and translations, and, on another, simply new copies of earlier ones'.[8] As Richard Sharpe noted in his recent and posthumously published Lyell Lectures, '[w]hile the iconography is always that of a writer

---

[5] Especially the outputs of the European Research Council–funded (2017–22) project Medieval Publishing from circa 1000 to 1500 (www.helsinki.fi/en/researchgroups/medieval-publishing).

[6] Riddy, '"Publication"', 30–7. The two modes of publication Riddy categorises as 'authorial' are 'the presentation by the author of a copy to a patron, and the public reading by an author of a new work to an audience' (ibid., 30). As Riddy points out, her treatment of the first of these modes owes much to Root's earlier work (ibid., 30–2).

[7] Niskanen, 'Authorial Culture', 72. Also compare S. Niskanen, *Publication and the Papacy in Late Antiquity and the Middle Ages* (Cambridge: Cambridge University Press, 2021), where (authorial) publishing is defined as 'a social act involving at base two parties: an author and their intended audience' (p. 1). Arguing in a similar vein more than a century earlier is R. K. Root, 'Publication before Printing', *PMLA*, 28 (1913), 417–31, especially 419–20.

[8] A. I. Doyle, 'Publication by Members of the Religious Orders', in J. Griffiths and D. Pearsall (eds.), *Book Production and Publishing in Britain, 1375–1475* (Cambridge: Cambridge University Press, 2007), pp. 109–23 (p. 110); my emphasis. Despite introducing this important caveat, most of Doyle's study is in fact concerned with authorial publishing.

composing, a true picture never encountered would depict a scribe copying with an exemplar open and the leaves of a new book in front of him'.[9] Indeed, in medieval monastic milieux, authorial publication was less common than, and secondary to, a different and primary mode of production, one which Riddy dubs 'official publishing', and which, in her definition, 'consists of the licensing of a work by an ecclesiastical authority'.[10] Both Riddy and Doyle primarily consider such official publications with regard to new compositions released and distributed for the first time under the license – and, in the age of print, with the imprimatur – of influential ecclesiastical individuals or institutions, usually from the ranks of the (archi)episcopate.[11] In medieval religious communities living in accordance with a monastic rule (*regula*), however, the licensing authority for the production, release, and dissemination (internal and external) of both authorial and non-authorial works ultimately lay with the domestic superior, normally an abbot or abbess.[12] As I will show in this Element, the narrow

[9] R. Sharpe, *Libraries and Books in Medieval England: The Role of Libraries in a Changing Book Economy. The Lyell Lectures for 2018–19*, ed. J. Willoughby (Oxford: Bodleian Library Publishing, 2023), p. 68.

[10] Riddy, '"Publication"', 30. Riddy's fourth mode of publication, which will not be discussed here, is that which 'relates to the role of metropolitan book-producers in the dissemination of texts', and which she labels 'commercial'. On commercial publishing in the Middle Ages, see R. H. Rouse and M. Rouse, *Manuscripts and Their Makers: Commercial Book Producers in Medieval Paris, 1200–1500* (Turnhout: Brepols, 2000); J. Griffiths and D. Pearsall (eds.), *Book Production and Publishing in Britain 1375–1475* (Cambridge: Cambridge University Press, 2007); Tether, *Publishing*, passim.

[11] Cases cited by Riddy, '"Publication"', 35–6, include Thomas Arundel, archbishop of York/Canterbury and Lord Chancellor (1386–9 and 1391–6), and William Grey, bishop of Ely (1454–78).

[12] On the role(s) of abbots and abbesses in medieval monastic book production, see B. Pohl, *Abbatial Authority and the Writing of History in the Middle Ages* (Oxford: Oxford University Press, 2023). In everyday practice, this overarching abbatial authority could be – and often was – delegated to various monastic officials such as priors, cantors/precentors, sacrists, librarians, and *armarii*; compare T. Webber, 'Cantor, Sacrist or Prior? The Provision of Books in Anglo-Norman England', in M. E. Fassler, K. A.-M. Bugyis, and A. B. Kraebel (eds.), *Medieval Cantors and Their*

definition of official publishing established by Riddy and Doyle for operating within the framework of authorial publication can be broadened, adapted, and applied beneficially in the context of twelfth-century monastic book production, licensing, release, and distribution as a hermeneutical key for unlocking the crucial role of the institutional superior.

Medievalists from various disciplines have called into question, and compellingly so, the perceived primacy of authors (and autographs) in the history of the medieval manuscript book, its production, and dissemination by drawing attention to the instrumental role of other publication agents such as scribes, editors, redactors, glossators, and commentators.[13] Even when accepting, as we should, that some of these agents acted in quasi-authorial capacities,[14] the fact remains that the vast majority of books made by medieval monastic communities and stored in their domestic libraries were *non*-authorial productions, even though many of them did contain authorial works. For the purposes of this study, authorial works shall be defined as those composed by an identifiable author, whilst authorial pub-

---

Craft: Music, Liturgy and the Shaping of History, 800–1500 (Woodbridge: Boydell, 2017), pp. 172–89.

[13] A. Minnis, *Medieval Theory of Authorship: Scholastic Literary Attitudes in the Later Middle Ages*, 2nd ed. (Philadelphia: University of Pennsylvania Press, 2010); I. Brügger Buddal and S. Rankovic (eds.), *Modes of Authorship in the Middle Ages* (Toronto: Pontifical Institute of Mediaeval Studies, 2012); J. F. Hamburger, *The Birth of the Author: Pictorial Prefaces in Glossed Books of the Twelfth Century* (Toronto: Pontifical Institute of Mediaeval Studies, 2021); L. Rösli and S. Gropper (eds.), *In Search of the Culprit: Aspects of Medieval Authorship* (Berlin: De Gruyter, 2021).

[14] See the cases studied by M. N. Fisher, *Scribal Authorship and the Writing of History in Medieval England* (Columbus: Ohio State University Press, 2012); E. Kennedy, 'The Scribe As Editor', in *Mélanges de langue et de littérature du Moyen Age et de la Renaissance offerts à Jean Frappier*, 2 vols. (Paris: Minard, 1970), vol. 1, pp. 523–31; J. T. Duggan, 'Turoldus, Scribe or Author? Evidence from the Corpus of Chansons de Geste', in Monica L. Wright, N. J. Lacy, and R. T. Pickens (eds.), *'Moult a sans et vallour': Studies in Medieval French Literature in Honor of William W. Kibler* (Amsterdam: Rodopi, 2012), pp. 135–44; L. Banella, 'Boccaccio As Anthologist and the Dawn of Editorial *Auctoritas*', *Mediaevalia*, 39 (2018), 275–97.

lication denotes, in Niskanen's useful definition, 'that crucial step from writer to reader taken to turn a *new* literary composition into a public commodity'.[15] Such new or original composition was comparatively rare in a monastic context, and most books on the shelves of monastic libraries and *armaria* were copies of existing works. This is true of the volumes one might expect to find in virtually every monastery irrespective of size and wealth because they were essential – and indeed indispensable – to the community's daily life and routine, chief amongst them books of Scripture and an at least basic stock of liturgical codices.[16] It also holds true for those that were, if not compulsory, regarded as canonical and owned by all but the smallest and poorest communities, and often in substantial numbers, first and foremost the writings of the Church Fathers, with Augustine, Gregory, and Jerome typically leading the charge.[17] It

[15] S. Niskanen, 'Authorial Publication in the Middle Ages', *Routledge Medieval Encyclopedia Online*, forthcoming; my emphasis. I am thankful to Samu Niskanen for sharing this article with me prior to its publication. A similar emphasis is placed by Jaakko Tahkokallio when defining authorial publication as 'making a new text available to an audience'; J. Tahkokallio, *The Anglo-Norman Historical Canon: Publishing and Manuscript Culture* (Cambridge: Cambridge University Press, 2019), p. 2.

[16] T. Webber, 'Monastic and Cathedral Book Collections in the Late Eleventh and Twelfth Centuries', in E. Leedham-Green and T. Webber (eds.), *The Cambridge History of Libraries in Britain and Ireland, Vol. I: To 1640* (Cambridge: Cambridge University Press, 2006), pp. 109–25; S. Boynton, 'The Bible and the Liturgy', in S. Boynton and D. J. Reilly (eds.), *The Practice of the Bible in the Middle Ages: Production, Reception, and Performance in Western Christianity* (New York: Columbia University Press, 2011), pp. 10–33; also the chapters by Teresa Webber ('The Libraries of Religious Houses'), Nicholas Bell ('Liturgical Books'), and Lesley Smith ('Books of Theology and Bible Study') in E. Kwakkel and R. M. Thomson (eds.), *The European Book in the Twelfth Century* (Cambridge: Cambridge University Press, 2018), pp. 103–21, 175–91, and 192–214.

[17] T. Webber, 'The Patristic Content of English Book Collections in the Eleventh Century: Toward a Continental Perspective', in P. R. Robinson and R. Zim (eds.), *Of the Making of Books: Medieval Manuscripts, Their Scribes and Readers. Essays presented to M. B. Parkes* (Aldershot: Ashgate, 1997), pp. 191–205; B. M. Kaczynski, 'The Authority of the Fathers: Patristic Texts in Early Medieval Libraries and Scriptoria', *Journal of Medieval Latin*, 16 (2006), 1–27; S. G. Bruce,

was *these* kinds of books, not authorial productions, that constituted the essence and substance of most monastic libraries in the Middle Ages.

Despite this preponderance of non-authorial productions in the libraries of medieval monastic houses, most scholarship has focused on authorial modes of publication.[18] This Element offers an alternative approach by concentrating specifically on non-authorial book production and the processes of licensing and authorisation involved therein, thereby entering into dialogue with recent research such as Niskanen's Element published in the same Gathering.[19] My vehicle for doing this will be a case study of a medieval monastery that witnessed a particular boost in domestic book production under the leadership of its twelfth-century abbots, thus leaving us with a sizeable corpus of manuscripts – many preserved in situ – to generate new and important insights into how abbatial authority shaped the entire process: the monastery of Engelberg in the Swiss Uri Alps that was founded in the early twelfth century in honour of the Virgin Mary.

'*Veterum vestigia patrum*: The Greek Patriarchs in the Manuscript Culture of Early Medieval Europe', *Downside Review*, 139 (2021), 6–23.

[18] For example, R. Sharpe, 'Anselm As Author: Publishing in the Late Eleventh Century', *Journal of Medieval Latin*, 19 (2009), 1–87; B. Pohl and L. Tether, 'Eadmer and His Books: A Case Study of Monastic Self-Publishing', in C. Rozier, S. N. Vaughn, and G. E. M. Gasper (eds.), *Eadmer of Canterbury: Historian, Hagiographer, and Theologian* (Leiden: Brill, forthcoming).

[19] Niskanen, *Publication*.

2 Engelberg's 'Scriptorium': What Do We Know?

Another concept that is essential to this Element – and to medieval manuscript culture – is that of the monastic scriptorium. Like *publishing*, the term *scriptorium* is highly evocative as it conjures visions of an organised, institutional writing workshop of significant size, often 'with its own set of surviving manuscripts, and a distinctive style of script practiced by multiple scribes';[20] using it routinely or indistinctly as a shorthand for monastic book production is problematic. As Rodney Thomson notes, '[o]ne question, perhaps too little considered, is the longevity of scriptoria', and '[t]he general rule seems to be that they lasted long enough to provide the basic stock for the library of the community. One or two generations of scribes might be sufficient to achieve this'.[21] Thomson adds nuance to the term's common definition as 'a locality where more than one scribe was at work, either contemporaneously or in succession', by reminding us that 'the mere fact of a number of scribes working in the same place simultaneously might not in itself constitute a scriptorium', which in addition requires 'a team of scribes under the discipline of a master, collaborating in the production of books'.[22] To what

---

[20] M. E. Fassler, 'Hildegard of Bingen and Her Scribes', in J. Bain (ed.), *The Cambridge Companion to Hildegard of Bingen* (Cambridge: Cambridge University Press, 2021), pp. 280–305 (p. 280), with reference to the workshop established at Disibodenberg by Hildegard of Bingen. M. Steinmann, 'Die Bücher des Abtes Frowin: Ein Skriptorium in Engelberg?', *Scriptorium*, 54 (2000), 9–13 (p. 11) likewise notes that '[i]n einem Skriptorium im vollen Sinn des Wortes wird Schreiben nach festen Regeln geübt und gelehrt, eine eigene Tradition entwickelt sich und wird weitegegeben'. See also M.-C. Garand, 'Le scriptorium de Guibert de Nogent', *Scriptorium*, 31 (1977), 3–29, on the workshop at Nogent-sous-Coucy. Workshops of comparable size existed at, for example, Montecassino and Michelsberg Abbey, Bamberg; F. L. Newton, *The Scriptorium and Library at Monte Cassino, 1058–1105* (Cambridge: Cambridge University Press, 1999); K. Dengler-Schreiber, *Scriptorium und Bibliothek des Klosters Michelsberg in Bamberg* (Graz: Akademische Druck- und Verlagsanstalt, 1979).

[21] R. M. Thomson, 'Scribes and Scriptoria', in E. Kwakkel and R. M. Thomson (eds.), *The European Book in the Twelfth Century* (Cambridge: Cambridge University Press, 2018), pp. 68–84 (p. 79).

[22] Thomson, 'Scribes', 76–8.

extent were these conditions – multiple scribes, distinctive house style, collaborative process, hierarchical organisation, and relative longevity – met at twelfth-century Engelberg?

Founded in 1120 by Conrad of Sellenbüren, a childless aristocrat, the Benedictine monastery of Engelberg in the canton of Obwalden (central Switzerland) within the diocese of Constance (but soon exempted from the *potestas* of its bishops) was one of the region's foremost centres of book production in the second half of the twelfth century.[23] The establishment and sustenance of this prolific scribal and artistic workshop despite the abbey's troubled early history was the achievement of three successive heads of house, Frowin (1143–78), Berchtold (1178–97), and Henry I (1197–1223).[24] Like many new monastic foundations, Engelberg does not seem to have had

---

[23] On Engelberg's foundation and early history, see F. Güterbock, *Engelbergs Gründung und erste Blüte, 1120–1223*, ed. G. Heer (Zurich: Leemann, 1948), pp. 5–31; H. Büchler-Mattmann and P. Heer, 'Die Benediktiner in der Schweiz: Engelberg OW', in E. Gilomen-Schenkel (ed.), *Frühe Klöster, die Benediktiner und Benediktinerinnen in der Schweiz* (Bern: Francke, 1986) [= *Helvetica Sacra* III/1.1], pp. 595–657; U. Hodel and R. De Kegel, 'Engelberg (Kloster)', in *Historisches Lexikon der Schweiz (HLS)*, https://hls-dhs-dss.ch/de/articles/008557/2011-03-31. The date of Engelberg's exemption has been the subject of some debate due to the contested authenticity of its earliest charters, including the 'foundation charter' (Engelberg, Stiftsarchiv, B.2; dated 2 November 1122) and the two confirmations issued in 1124 by Pope Calixtus II (Engelberg, Stiftsarchiv, A.1) and Emperor Henry V (Engelberg, Stiftsarchiv, B.1), respectively; E. G. Vogel, 'Urkunden des Stiftes Engelberg', *Der Geschichtsfreund: Mitteilungen des Historischen Vereins Zentralschweiz*, 49 (1894), 235–62 (pp. 235–43 = nos. 2–4).

[24] *Die Bilderwelt des Klosters Engelberg: Das Skriptorium unter den Äbten Frowin (1143–1178), Bechtold (1178–1197) and Heinrich (1197–1223)*, ed. C. Eggenberger (Luzern: Diopter, 1999); M. Steinmann, 'Abt Frowin von Engelberg (1143–1178) und seine Handschriften', *Der Geschichtsfreund: Mitteilungen des Historischen Vereins Zentralschweiz*, 146 (1993), 7–36; H. Feiss, 'Frowin of Engelberg: His Monastery, His Scriptorium, and His Books', *American Benedictine Review*, 56 (2005) 68–99 and 194–212; R. Durrer, 'Die Schreiber- und Malerschule von Engelberg', *Anzeiger für Schweizerische Altertumskunde*, 3 (1901), 42–55 and 122–60; W. Hafner, 'Die Maler- und Schreiberschule von Engelberg', *Stultifera navis*, 11 (1954), 13–20.

a scriptorium from the outset. Judging from the surviving evidence, the contents of its initial book collection – nothing indicates a fully fledged library at this early stage – of mostly liturgical codices and, presumably, a copy of the *Rule of St Benedict* were produced elsewhere and brought to Engelberg by its first 'abbot', Adelhelm (1120–31).[25] Adelhelm came to Engelberg from Muri, and it is entirely plausible that the basic stock of books he carried with him to help support his new monastery's daily routine either came from Muri's library or had been copied there from domestic exemplars prior to Adelhelm's departure – practices that were not uncommon amongst founding abbots charged with creating new communities and furnishing them with book collections ex nihilo.[26] There is, to my knowledge, no

---

[25] A. Bruckner (ed.), *Scriptoria medii aevi Helvetica, Vol. VIII: Schreibschulen der Diözese Konstanz, Stift Engelberg* (Geneva: Roto-Sadag, 1950), pp. 14–18; compare Feiss, 'Frowin', 84; Steinmann, 'Bücher', 10. Engelberg's earliest extant copy of the *Rule of St Benedict* (Engelberg, Stiftsbibliothek, MS Cod. 72) dates from the second half of the thirteenth century; see B. M. von Scarpatetti (ed.), *Katalog der datierten Handschriften in der Schweiz in lateinischer Schrift vom Anfang des Mittelalters bis 1550, Vol. II: Die Handschriften der Bibliotheken Bern-Porrentruy* (Zurich: Graf, 1983), pp. 92–3 (no. 251). Whether the eleventh-century canon-law codex of uncertain origin (Engelberg, Stiftsbibliothek, MS Cod. 52) and/or the ninth-century copy of Hildemar of Corbie's commentary on the *Rule of St Benedict* from Reichenau (Engelberg, Stiftsbibliothek, MS Cod. 142) really formed part of this initial collection as asserted confidently by Bruckner seems questionable; *Catalogus codicum manu scriptorum qui asservantur in Bibliotheca Monasterii O.S.B. Engelbergensis in Helvetia*, ed. B. Gottwald (Freiburg i. Br.: Typis Herderianis, 1891), pp. 89–90 and 145; W. Hafner, *Der Basiliuskommentar zur Regula S. Benedicti: Ein Beitrag zur Autorenfrage karolingischer Regelkommentare* (Münster: Aschendorff, 1959), pp. 7–9. As noted by Güterbock, *Gründung*, 6 and 22, Adelhelm carries the title *prior* ('prior') – rather than *abbot* ('abbas') – in the earliest documentary sources, perhaps indicating the monastery's initial dependency on Muri and its abbots.

[26] Various examples are discussed in Pohl, *Abbatial Authority*. On Muri's library and scriptorium, see *Katalog der mittelalterlichen Handschriften der Klöster Muri und Hermetschwil*, ed. C. Bretscher-Gisiger and R. Gamper (Zurich: Graf, 2005), pp. 13–22.

evidence of in-house book production at Engelberg for Adelhelm's abbacy, and the same is true for his direct successor(s).

In Adelhelm's case, this lack of domestic scribal activity can probably be explained through a combination of related factors. To begin with, his managerial attention and the resources at his disposal in the years following the community's foundation presumably had to be devoted to other, more pressing fields of activity that took precedence over the production of books, especially if the fledgling community had indeed been supplied with the most essential volumes by the mother house at Muri. These priorities included, first and foremost, the cultivation and expansion of the monastic demesne in a naturally resourceful if remote locality in the Alpine foothills that had been prepared for human settlement and agriculture but required further development – and investment – to sustain even an initial allocation of twelve or so monks.[27] Substantial though Conrad's foundational gift had been, it nevertheless required Adelhelm to launch a targeted acquisition policy ('gezielte Erwerbspolitik') that involved considerable resources and was continued by his successors.[28] With property enlargement and the consolidation of abbatial lordship at the forefront of Engelberg's early government strategy, promoting the abbey's cultural and literary profile with books for non-canonical reading, teaching, and study initially seems to have taken a back seat. Whether this single-mindedness in the early phases of the community's existence was due purely to pragmatism on Adelhelm's part or at least partly a result of external pressure – perhaps by the founding patron, Conrad, whose continued involvement and eventual retirement (1126) at Engelberg may have had some influence on the policies of its first abbot, or by the abbots of Muri, who might not have relished the prospect of being rivalled culturally by

[27] Güterbock, *Gründung*, 9–12; Steinmann, 'Frowin', 7–8; Büchler-Mattmann and Heer, 'Engelberg', 598–9. On the likely size of Engelberg's twelfth-century community, see below in this chapter. The common size of new monastic foundations (twelve monks plus an abbot) was meant to resemble the community of Christ and his apostles.

[28] Büchler-Mattmann and Heer, 'Engelberg', 598.

a daughter house at the outskirts of their own demesne – is impossible to know.[29]

That external forces could have a profound impact on the community's governance and stifle its development became evident under Adelhelm's immediate successors, who had their names erased (temporarily) from memory by the compiler(s) of the *Annales Engelbergenses maiores* and were shunned as *ababbates* – a derogatory medieval Latin neologism that evades straightforward translation into English but denotes perversion and abomination of the abbatial office.[30] Thanks to the fifteenth-century *Annales Engelbergenses minores*, we know that they were called Lu(i)tfried, Welfo, and Hesso.[31] Far from rehabilitating their legacy, however, the later medieval chronicler likewise styles them as agents of evil ('male praefuerunt') who were hateful to God ('Deo odibiles'), lived odiously ('indigne vixerunt'), and

---

[29] Bruckner's assertions that Adelhelm was keen on promoting the nascent community's intellectual life ('bedacht auf das religiose und geistige Leben des Klosters') and likely considered the creation of a scriptorium to help build a well-stocked domestic library ('dass Adelhelm ebenfalls an die Schaffung eines Scriptoriums und einer breiten Bibliothek dachte') are based on analogies with the first abbot of Muri, Reginbold, in whom Brucker sees – perhaps wishfully – a close parallel; Bruckner (ed.), *Scriptoria*, 15 and 17.

[30] Engelberg, Stiftsbibliothek, MS Cod. 9, fols. 1 r–10 v; edited as 'Annales Engelbergenses, a.1147–1546', in *Annales aevi Suevici* [= *MGH SS* XVII], ed. G. H. Pertz (Hanover: Hahn, 1861), pp. 278–82 (p. 278). Güterbock, *Gründung*, 76–9, ascribes the omission of their names to a thirteenth-century redactor, but the palaeography of Sarnen, Benediktinerkollegium, MS Cod. membr. 10 – the *Annales*'s earliest extant recension unavailable to Güterbock – speaks against this. As a result of this *damnatio memoriae*, the official succession narrative leapfrogs these 'ababbates' by jumping from Adelhelm to Frowin, who in the *Annales* is presented as Engelberg's second abbot ('secundus abbas'). On the term *ababbas, -atis*, compare '*ababbas, m.', in *Mittellateinisches Wörterbuch*, ed. O. Prinz and H. Gneuss, 7 vols. (Munich: Beck, 1967–99), vol. 1, p. 5 (www.woerterbuchnetz.de/MLW/*ababbas).

[31] Edited by P. Tanner, 'Die ältesten Jahrbücher Engelbergs', *Der Geschichtsfreund: Mitteilungen des Historischen Vereins Zentralschweiz*, 8 (1852), 101–17 (pp. 108–13, at p. 109).

over the course of a decade almost bankrupted the community by selling and alienating its properties ('bona monasterii dilapidaverunt').[32] Based on a charter issued in 1143 by Pope Innocent II that prohibits anyone from seizing the monastery by force, Hugh Feiss suspects that none of them had been freely elected by the community,[33] perhaps indicating that they were 'planted' and controlled by external (most likely secular) powers. That said, the parallels between these complaints by Engelberg's domestic annalists and those in the roughly contemporary *Acta Murensia* noted by Ferdinand Güterbock, and the fact that one of Adelhelm's dishonoured successors shares his name with Luitfried, abbot of Muri (1085–96), may just allow for the possibility that these three men were imposed on Engelberg's monks by Muri, their former mother house and Adelhelm's sometime home institution.[34] Whatever their origins and the extent of the damage they caused at Engelberg, Albert Bruckner's conclusion that under these *ababbates* the basic conditions for establishing a well-organised and functioning scriptorium were lacking is compelling.[35] For these facilities to be built, it took the initiative of the next abbot: Frowin (1143–78).

Frowin too came to Engelberg as an outsider, though unlike Adelhelm – and, if Güterbock's suspicion is correct, Luitfried, Welfo, and Hesso – he had been a monk not of Muri, but of St Blasien in the Black Forest.[36] Like Adelhelm, Frowin upon his abbatial appointment also seems to have brought some books with him from his previous home. And just like

---

[32] Tanner, 'Jahrbücher', 109.

[33] Feiss, 'Frowin', 76. Innocent II's charter is edited in Vogel, 'Urkunden', 243–4 (no. 5).

[34] Güterbock, *Gründung*, 28–9. Also compare H. Hirsch, 'Die *Acta Murensia* und die ältesten Urkunden des Klosters Muri', *Mitteilungen des Instituts für Österreichische Geschichtsforschung*, 25 (1904), 209–74.

[35] Bruckner (ed.), *Scriptoria*, 17: '[Es] fehlen für eine organisierte[,] gutarbeitende Schreibschule . . . alle günstigen Voraussetzungen'.

[36] On Frowin's biography and career, see R. De Kegel, 'Frowin', in *Historisches Lexikon der Schweiz (HLS)* (https://hls-dhs-dss.ch/de/articles/012646/2006-01-09); L. Hunkeler, 'Frowin als Mönch und Abt', in *Der selige Frowin von Engelberg, 1143–1178* (Engelberg: Stiftsdruckerei, 1943), pp. 7–17; Güterbock, *Gründung*, 33–5 and 40–3.

those imported from Muri in 1120, the volumes arriving from St Blasien with Frowin in 1143 included liturgical codices like an antiphonal redis-covered in 1963 under the floorboards of a monk's cell alongside nine other volumes previously presumed lost that had been stashed away for safe-keeping, presumably during the abbey's occupation by French soldiers in 1798.[37] This time, however, the primary motivation for importing books for the liturgy and monastic observance was not provision ex nihilo, but replacement and reform of what was already there.[38] What is more, Frowin within a few years of his arrival established a monastic school at Engelberg. One of the volumes unearthed in 1963 (Engelberg, Stiftsbibliothek, MS Cod. 1007, a copy of Gregory the Great's *Homilies*) contains an inventory (fol. 114 r) of books used regularly (if not exclusively) for teaching, from classical works by Prudentius, Priscian, Statius, Cicero, and the *Ilias Latina* to early medieval writers such as Boethius and Paschasius Radbertus, and even recently composed – and indeed contemporary – texts like the teachings of Peter the Chanter.[39] Some of these may well have come from St Blasien, either as part of Frowin's initial provision or in subsequent instalments, whereas others were almost certainly produced in-house from exemplars borrowed from St Blasien, Einsiedeln, and perhaps elsewhere, providing us with the earliest evidence of domestic book production at Engelberg.[40] Just how big an operation was this, though?

---

[37] W. Hafner, 'Die Engelberger Bücherfunde', *Librarium*, 6 (1963), 113–18 (p. 117); also compare G. Muff, 'Die Stiftsbibliothek Engelberg: Einhundertundzwanzigtausend Werke – neun davon im Fussboden', *Musik und Liturgie*, 135 (2010), 4–8; Steinmann, 'Frowin', 21–2.

[38] Compare Hunkeler, 'Frowin', 11–15.

[39] P. Lehmann, 'Das wiedergefundene älteste Bücherverzeichnis des Benediktinerstiftes Engelberg', *Sitzungsberichte der Bayerischen Akademie der Wissenschaften, Philosophisch-Historische Abteilung*, 1964/IV (1964) [= *Beiträge zur mittelalterlichen Bibliotheks- und Überlieferungsgeschichte* I], 5–7; previously edited (prior to the original inventory's rediscovery) in *Mittelalterliche Bibliothekskataloge Deutschlands und der Schweiz*, ed. P. Lehmann, P. Ruf, C. E. Ineichen-Eder, et al., 4 vols. (Munich: Beck, 1918–2009), vol. 1, pp. 30–3 (no. 10).

[40] Feiss, 'Frowin', 86–7; Steinmann, 'Frowin', 25–6.

According to a petition brought before Pope Innocent III circa 1199 to secure additional revenues for the sustenance of Engelberg's growing community, the abbey at that point included forty monks plus eighty nuns ('[h]ic xl monachi iugiter in Dei laudibus perseverant; illinc sanctimoniales lxxx').[41] Precise numbers also exist for 1330/1 thanks to an inquest conducted at the command of Einsiedeln's abbot, Engelberg's then governor, according to which the community comprised twenty individuals (including the abbot and a pair of novices), but not for the early decades after the abbey's foundation.[42] A conservative estimate projected backwards from a period of steady growth and expansion under Abbots Berchtold and Henry would seem to suggest that at the time of Frowin's abbacy, certainly during its early years, the community cannot have been substantially larger than it had been at the end of Adelhelm's tenure, perhaps comprising somewhere between one and two dozen monks. To find in a community of such relatively young age and moderate size an experienced, well-trained scribe (let alone several) was by no means a given, and having the resources and personnel available domestically to assemble a workshop deserving of the term *scriptorium* an exception.

In response to some rather optimistic assessments in previous scholarship, Martin Steinmann argues persuasively that the domestic production of books under Frowin was essentially the work of a small team of four or fewer regular scribes who sometimes operated by themselves, and other times in tandem.[43] As there are no traces of their scribal work at Engelberg prior to Frowin's arrival in 1143, it seems possible and plausible that they came with him from St Blasien.[44] Contrary to traditional portrayals of Frowin as the founder of not just a scribal workshop ('Schreiber*stube*'), but a formal scribal

---

[41] Edited by P. Delius, 'Urkundenlese aus dem Lande Unterwalden, ob und nid dem Wald: von 1148 bis 1512', *Der Geschichtsfreund: Mitteilungen des Historischen Vereins Zentralschweiz*, 14 (1858), 234–69 (pp. 236–7 = no. 3), with a regest in Vogel, 'Urkunden', 260 (no. 21); also compare Güterbock, *Gründung*, 61; Feiss, 'Frowin', 81.

[42] Büchler-Mattmann and Heer, 'Engelberg', 597.

[43] Steinmann, 'Frowin', 28–9, who subsequently reduces this estimate even further to just three scribes; see Steinmann, 'Bücher', 11.

[44] Bruckner (ed.), *Scriptoria*, 20 and 29–30.

school ('Schreiber*schule*'),[45] Steinmann's critical reassessment suggests more of an ad hoc operation, one in which the production of books was achieved collaboratively by a task force of individuals surrounding the abbot, each with his own specific area(s) of responsibility and expertise.[46] One was the so-called schoolmaster ('Schulmeister'; his real name is unknown) placed in charge of the monks' education, who helped copy and correct some of the volumes listed on the aforementioned inventory, including a copy of Cicero's *De inventione* (Engelberg, Stiftsbibliothek, MS Cod. 154), and who perhaps acted as the abbot's *secretarius*.[47] Another member of Frowin's workforce, the only one besides Frowin known by name, was Richene, a monk-copyist whose expert penmanship crafted the three-volume *Engelberg Bible* (Engelberg, Stiftsbibliothek, MSS Cod. 3–5), and whose career has been traced back to St Blasien.[48] It is not impossible, and perhaps likely, that there were others both inside and outside the community (possibly including professional scribes) who occasionally lent a hand in the production of manuscripts under Frowin. Until the entire corpus is subjected to comprehensive palaeographical analysis, however, an undertaking that lies outside

---

[45] E. Omlin, 'Abt Frowin als Gründer der Engelberger Schreiberschule', in *Der selige Frowin von Engelberg, 1143–1178* (Engelberg: Stiftsdruckerei, 1943), pp. 26–35 and 47–53 (p. 26); Hafner, 'Schreiberschule', 14; Bruckner (ed.), *Scriptoria*, 19–20.

[46] Steinmann, 'Bücher', 11–12: 'Ein Skriptorium im Sinn einer feste Konventionen schaffenden Gemeinschaft jedenfalls gab es [in Engelberg] nicht'.

[47] Steinmann, 'Bücher', 12; Steinmann, 'Frowin', 25–6. On the role of monastic *secretarii* in the production of books, see M.-C. Garand, *Guibert de Nogent et ses secretaires* (Turnhout: Brepols, 1995); V. Gazeau, 'Du *secretarius* au secretaire: Remarques sur un office médiéval méconnu', in L. Jégou, S. Joye, T. Lienhard, et al. (eds.), *Faire lien: Aristocratie, réseaux et échanges compétitifs* (Paris: Publications de la Sorbonne, 2015), pp. 63–72.

[48] Bruckner (ed.), *Scriptoria*, 23 and 54; Steinmann, 'Frowin', 14–16; R. Bonifazi, 'Die beiden Miniaturen der Frowin-Bibel auf Einzelblättern', in C. Eggenberger (ed.), *Die Bilderwelt des Klosters Engelberg: Das Skriptorium unter den Äbten Frowin (1143–1178), Bechtold (1178–1197) and Heinrich (1197–1223)* (Luzern: Diopter, 1999), pp. 27–30; the model – and perhaps exemplar(s) – of the *Engelberg Bible* might have come from Einsiedeln; see Feiss, 'Frowin', 88.

the scope of this Element, those identifiable with sufficient certainty and regularity remain Richene, the schoolmaster, an anonymous copyist, versifier, and rubricator (see Chapter 3), and Frowin.[49] Our main interest here lies with the individual whose rank and authority were second to none inside the monastery, and who – as the following chapters will argue – was the primary agent in the community's book production: Abbot Frowin.

---

[49] Steinmann, 'Frowin', 16. Also see Chapter 3 on Frowin's first-hand scribal activity.

3 Colophons: What's in a Name?

As others have observed, most of the books made at Engelberg under Abbot Frowin still extant today exhibit colophons that mention him by name. By my own count, no fewer than thirty-six of the forty surviving volumes (90 per cent) have them, and they are transcribed, translated, and numbered (nos. 1–36) in the Appendix of this Element for reference.[50] As Steinmann notes, about two thirds are the product of a single hand, the same hand that wrote the book list in MS Engelberg 1007.[51] Their intended function has been the subject of some speculation and will be discussed further in Chapter 4. For now, let us focus on what the colophons actually say.

All thirty-six colophons are composed in verse. More specifically, they are Leonine verses – a mnemonically highly effective combination of metrical structure (typically hexameters) and internal rhyme (usually between the final syllable and the syllable before the caesura/penthemimeres) suitable for aural modes of recital and reception that rose to prominence across the Latin West in the eleventh and twelfth centuries.[52]

---

[50] A seventeenth-century inventory of Engelberg's monastic library (Vatican, Archivio Apostolico Vaticano, Fondo Bolognetti 332) includes transcriptions of some of these colophons; edited in Bruckner (ed.), *Scriptoria*, 89–103. A selection was also printed by H. von Liebenau, *Versuch einer urkundlichen Darstellung des reichsfreien Stiftes Engelberg, St. Benedikten-Ordens in der Schweiz: Zwölftes und dreizehntes Jahrhundert* (Luzern: Räber, 1846), pp. 34 n. 2–4 and 35–6 n. 1–4; more were added by the editors of *Colophons de manuscrits occidentaux des origines au XVIe siécle*, ed. Bénédictins de Bouveret, 6 vols. (Fribourg, CH: Éditions Universitaires, 1965–82), vol. 2; Bruckner (ed.), *Scriptoria*, 107–30; and Von Scarpatetti (ed.), *Katalog*, vol. 2. Omlin, 'Frowin', 47–50, n. 3–72, identified twenty-seven colophons without knowledge of the books rediscovered in 1963; Steinmann, 'Frowin', 16–17, counts thirty-four across as many volumes, as does Feiss, 'Frowin', 85.

[51] See Steinmann, 'Frowin', 12–13 and 26–7, with the intriguing suggestion that this hand might in fact belong to the abbey's librarian/*armarius* who – by virtue of his office and the authority invested in him by the abbot – would have constituted an important publication agent in his own right.

[52] J. Haynes, 'Leonine Verse', in C. M. Furey, J. M. LeMon, B. Matz, et al. (eds.), *Encyclopedia of the Bible and Its Reception*, 21 vols. (Berlin: De Gruyter, 2009–23),

They are all original compositions, and with two exceptions (nos. 21 and 30; nos. 5, 24, and 28), no two are identical, though some represent variations of each other (nos. 3 and 33; nos. 6 and 27; nos. 31 and 34) or 'riff' on common themes (nos. 8, 10, 16, 18, and 26).[53] Beginning with some of the shortest and most straightforward verses, they consist of a single hexameter describing Frowin in the function(s) of the books' commissioner and/or presenter, frequently (but not always) in figurative juxtaposition or fictive dialogue with a saint. Good examples of this are no. 35 ('Abbot Frowin had this book made') and the offerings to Christ and Mary in nos. 7 and 31, respectively. As the abbey's patron saint, Mary features prominently in the corpus, with no fewer than ten verses (28 per cent) dedicated explicitly to her (nos. 4a, 5, 11, 15, 23, 24, 28, 31, 34, and 36), and three to Christ (nos. 4b, 7, and 25). I return to Mary later in this chapter. Another prominent dedicatee represented by four verses – second only to Mary – is the monastic community (nos. 3, 14, 26, and 32). What renders these colophons of particular significance is that they address Frowin in the vocative ('Frowine') as if to remind him that it was he who had arranged for these volumes to be made ('fecisti'; 'de scriptura fuit tibi cura') and given (out) to the monks ('dedisti'; 'tribuisti'). It is tempting to imagine that these are not just symbolic words, but witnesses to a real performative practice of physically presenting books made in-house to the abbot for authorisation prior to their incorporation into the abbey's library. This sequence of handovers – first from the scribe(s) to the commissioning abbot, and then from the abbot to the community – constituted, I contend, an act of *publication*, one in which books made in-house were officially authorised for release to and consumption by a *public* that comprised, in the first instance, the monastic community

vol. 16, pp. 128–9; D. L. Norberg and J. M. Ziolkowski, *An Introduction to the Study of Medieval Latin Versification* (Washington, DC: Catholic University of America Press, 2004), p. 40; C. Brooks, *Reading Medieval Latin Poetry Aloud: A Practical Guide to Two Thousand Years of Verse* (Cambridge: Cambridge University Press, 2007), p. 286.

[53] Note that nos. 5, 24, and 28 have further parallels in nos. 41 and 44, both produced under Frowin's successor, Berchtold. On Berchtold's verses, see Chapter 4.

itself and, in a second and broader sense, external users with fairly regular (if carefully controlled) access to Engelberg's domestic library.[54]

In a monastic community like Engelberg, the production of books was subject to the superior's permission and approval. For each volume, singular provision had to be made, a capable workforce assembled, tasks assigned, materials resourced, time carved out from the daily routine, and licence granted, typically on a case-by-case basis.[55] The *Rule of St Benedict* stipulates that monks must not be given writing or bookmaking implements without abbatial permission, 'no book, no wax tablets, no stylus, nothing whatsoever' ('neque codicem, neque tabulas, neque graphium, sed nihil omnino'), at the same time as obliging the abbot to keep a list of whatever is distributed and allocated with his authorisation.[56] Similar stipulations are found in monastic customaries produced across the Latin West from the eleventh century onwards. The twelfth-century *Liber ordinis* of Saint-Victor in Paris states that scribes internal to the community must be assigned and authorised by the abbot before they can be issued any writing tools and materials by the *armarius*.[57] As the abbot's delegate, the *armarius* is strictly forbidden from giving any work to scribes without abbatial permission.[58]

---

[54] On this notion of publication, compare Sharpe, 'Anselm', 1, n. 2.

[55] The procedures, provisions, and personnel involved are discussed in Pohl, *Abbatial Authority*.

[56] *The Rule of St Benedict*, ed./tr. B. L. Venarde (Cambridge, MA: Harvard University Press, 2011), pp. 122–3. Similar stipulations are also found in other monastic rules, including the *Rule of the Master*; see *La Régle du Maître*, ed./tr. A. de Vogüé, 3 vols. (Paris: Éditions du Cerf, 1964), vol. 2, pp. 78–9.

[57] On the *armarius*, see R. Sharpe, 'The Medieval Librarian', in E. Leedham-Green and T. Webber (eds.), *The Cambridge History of Libraries in Britain and Ireland, Vol. I: To 1640* (Cambridge: Cambridge University Press, 2006), pp. 218–41.

[58] *Liber ordinis Sancti Victoris Parisiensis*, ed. L. Jocqué and L. Milis (Turnhout: Brepols, 1984), pp. 79–80: 'Quicumque de fratribus intra claustrum scriptores sunt, et quibus officium scribendi ab abbate iniunctum est, omnibus his armarius providere debet ... Ceteros autem fratres, qui scribere sciunt, et tamen officium scribendi eis iniunctum non est, sine licentia abbatis ad scribendum ponere armarius non debet.' Should the *armarius* wish to employ scribes not assigned by the abbot, he must indicate this to him first ('prius abbati indicare debet') and

The late eleventh-century *Consuetudines Cluniacenses* also prohibit Cluny's *armarius* from giving work to the abbey's scribes without permission from the abbot or prior ('nisi abbatis, aut prioris licentia') for whom he acts as deputy ('vicarius').[59] The eleventh-century *Constitutiones Hirsaugienses* from Hirsau and the *Liber tramitis* from Farfa are both in agreement that monks should only be excused from communal duties – including Mass – to undertake scribal work with the abbot's special dispensation ('per licentiam domni abbatis').[60] Nobody, the General Chapter of Canterbury concluded in 1277, may write or illuminate books of any kind without abbatial licence or ask others to do so.[61] Making books without – or worse, against – their abbot's mandate could have serious consequences for the monks involved, from private admonition and public castigation in the chapter to removal from office and corporal punishment such as whipping and the withholding of food.[62]

It is important to note that these and similar stipulations apply not only to new compositions, but also – and of primary interest to the present

obtain his licence to commission what is agreed ('per eius licentiam et praeceptum facere, quod faciendum est'), but nothing else ('[n]ullus autem praeter id, quod sibi iniunctum est, sine licentia abbatis scribere praesumat').

[59] 'Ordo Cluniacensis', ed. M. Hergott, in *Vetus disciplina monastica* (Paris: Osmont, 1726; repr. Siegburg: Schmitt, 1999), pp. 136–364 (p. 161). On the date (c.1080) of the *Consuetudines* written by Bernard of Cluny, see I. Cochelin, 'Customaries As Inspirational Sources', in C. Marino Malone and C. Maines (eds.), Consuetudines et Regulae: *Sources for Monastic Life in the Middle Ages and the Early Modern Period* (Turnhout: Brepols, 2014), pp. 27–72 (pp. 56–7); also I. Cochelin, 'Discipline and the Problem of Cluny's Customaries', in S. G. Bruce and S. Vanderputten (eds.), *A Companion to the Abbey of Cluny in the Middle Ages* (Leiden: Brill, 2021), pp. 204–22 (p. 206).

[60] *Willehelmi Abbatis Constitutiones Hirsaugienses*, ed. P. Engelbert and C. Elvert, 2 vols. (Siegburg: Schmitt, 2010), vol. 1, p. 68; *Liber tramitis aevi Odilonis abbatis*, ed. P. Dinter (Siegburg: Schmitt, 1980), pp. 219 and 227.

[61] *Documents Illustrating the Activities of the General and Provincial Chapters of the English Black Monks, 1215–1540*, ed. W. A. Pantin, 3 vols. (London: Royal Historical Society, 1931–7), vol. 1, p. 74 (no. 28).

[62] See the examples studied in Pohl, *Abbatial Authority*.

discussion – to the copying of existing works. As noted in the Introduction, most books copied and collected in medieval monasteries fall into the latter category, and Engelberg is no exception. All but two of the volumes manufactured under Frowin are non-authorial productions – the sole exceptions being Frowin's own compositions, the *Explanatio Dominicae orationis* (Einsiedeln, Stiftsbibliothek, MS Cod. 240 (641)) and *De laude liberi arbitrii libri septem* (Engelberg, Stiftsbibliothek, MS Cod. 46).[63] Augustine and Gregory feature most prominently with twelve (30 per cent) and six (15 per cent) volumes, respectively, followed by Bernard of Clairvaux (six volumes), Jerome (three), and Ambrose (two).[64] The fact that Augustine is the second most cited authority in the *Explanatio* and *De laude* – second only to the Bible! – has led to the suggestion that Frowin had his works copied for personal use, rather than for the monastic library.[65] This seems rather implausible, however, given that by the twelfth century patristic author(itie)s such as Augustine and Gregory formed a staple of monastic libraries across the Latin West.[66] Of

---

[63] *Frowinus de Monte Angelorum: Explanatio Dominicae orationis. Additus Tractatus de veritate*, ed. S. Beck and R. De Kegel (Turnhout: Brepols, 1998); O. Bauer, *Frowin von Engelberg (1147–1178)*, *'De laude liberi arbitrii libri septem': Versuch einer literatischen und theologiegeschichtlichen Bestimmung der Handschrift 46 von Engelberg* (Louvain: Abbaye du Mont César, 1948). Also compare Feiss, 'Frowin', 194–201.

[64] St Augustine: Engelberg, Stiftsbibliothek, MSS Cod. 12–18, 87–9, 138, and 1008; St Gregory: Engelberg, Stiftsbibliothek, MSS Cod. 19–23, and 1007; St Bernard: Engelberg, Stiftsbibliothek, MSS Cod. 32–4, 89, and 139; St Jerome: Engelberg, Stiftsbibliothek, MSS Cod. 48, 49 and 76; and St Ambrose: Engelberg, Stiftsbibliothek, MSS Cod. 64 and 65.

[65] Steinmann, 'Frowin', 26; also compare Feiss, 'Frowin', 195–7 and 200, noting that 'Augustine is cited by name over 200 times [in *De laude*]. Frowin quotes from 40 of Augustine's works. One quarter of *De laude* consists of Augustine's words' (p. 197).

[66] See Kaczynski, 'Authority'; Webber, 'Patristic Content'; T. Webber, 'The Diffusion of Augustine's *Confessions* in England during the Eleventh and Twelfth Centuries', in J. Blair and B. Golding (eds.), *The Cloister and the World: Essays in Honour of Barbara Harvey* (Oxford: Oxford University Press, 1996), pp. 29–45.

Figure 1 Frowin presenting a book to the Virgin Mary (and Christ)
Engelberg, Stiftsbibliothek, MS Cod. 3, fol. 1 v, reproduced with permission

the four volumes dedicated explicitly to Engelberg's monks, two are works by Gregory (MS Engelberg 20: part one of the *Moralia in Iob*; MS Engelberg 1007: *Homilia*) and one contains Augustine's *De doctrina Christiana* (MS Engelberg 87), and there is evidence that other works by these authors were also intended for use by the monastic community. The colophon in part two of the *Moralia* (MS Engelberg 21; no. 15) states that Frowin ordered the book because it nurtures the monk's mind ('noverit pascere mentem'), whilst that in part three (MS Engelberg 22; no. 16) praises Frowin for providing a tool to help teach the hidden secrets of Christ to the monks; the colophon in Augustine's *Enarrationes in Psalmos* (MS Engelberg 12; no. 8) addresses the reader directly, and that in *De civitate Dei* (MS Engelberg 1008; no. 33) recalls that Frowin gave the book for the faithful to read. In each case, the expectation expressed in the book's colophon is one of communal rather than personal usage.

Complementing this basic publication process (scribe > abbot > community) are ten colophons that have Mary acting as intercessor and interlocutor between the abbot and the community. Five times Frowin personally approaches the patron saint to present her with a book (nos. 4a, 5, 23, 24, and 28; Figure 1), and five times he is described as doing so in the third person (nos. 11, 15, 31, 34, and 36).[67] The books' real recipient is not Mary herself, of course, but the monastic community founded in her name: by accepting the books intended for communal usage and consumption from Frowin, Mary endorses their release and provision to the monks. This is not to suggest that we should dismiss her prominent inclusion and repeated naming in the colophons as mere lip service. Rather than playing a passive part, Mary assumes an active role alongside Frowin, effectively co-governing the community with the abbot and reinforcing his authority by adding hers to it. Frowin's authority depends on the patron saint's agency, and there was an expectation of mutual

---

[67] On the miniature in no. 4a, see Bonifazi, 'Miniaturen', 28; K. Zogg, 'Maria, Adams Rippe und die verbotene Frucht', in C. Eggenberger (ed.), *Die Bilderwelt des Klosters Engelberg: Das Skriptorium unter den Äbten Frowin (1143–1178), Bechtold (1178–1197) and Heinrich (1197–1223)* (Luzern: Diopter, 1999), pp. 21–6 (p. 25).

support. Nowhere is this expectation expressed more clearly and vividly than in a prayer composed by Anselm, abbot of Le Bec (1078–93) and archbishop of Canterbury (1093–1109). Written in the voice of a self-castigating prelate (an abbot or bishop), the prayer beseeches the unnamed patron saint to act as the superior's helper and advocate:

> I, I say, whom God and you after God,
> either ordered or permitted (I know not which)
> to be called abbot of this church under your patronage ('sub te advocato')
> under your leadership ('sub te tutore'), constituted under your name;
> anxious about myself and those committed to me,
> I beg to consult you ('te rogo consultorem'),
> I pray you to listen ('te precor adiutorem'),
> and I expect you through all to work on my behalf ('pro me operatorem').[68]

Similar to Mary's role in the aforementioned colophons, the patron saint's task as described in Anselm's prayer is to mediate between the abbot and the community of monks entrusted to him:

> So holy, blessed, and good N., recognise me
> as in some kind of way your deputy ('vicarium tuum'),
> and always go before me ('praeveniat') with your counsel,
> and follow me ('subsequatur') with your help,
> ruling me, and the flock committed to me
> ('ad regendum me ipsum et gregem mihi commissum').
> For they are committed more to you than to me,
> and those who are committed to me
> are not taken away from you,

---

[68] 'Oratio episcopi vel abbatis ad sanctum sub cuius nomine regit ecclesiam', in *Sancti Anselmi Cantuariensis archiepiscopi opera omnia*, ed. F. S. Schmitt, 6 vols. (Edinburgh: Nelson & Sons, 1938–61), vol. 3, pp. 68–70 (p. 68) (no. 17). Translated in *The Prayers and Meditations of Saint Anselm*, tr. B. Ward (New York: Penguin, 1973), pp. 207–11 (p. 207).

but I am the more greatly committed to you.
So what is enjoined upon me about them
do you perform for me and for them ('tu fac de me et de illis').
Do on my behalf what is enjoined upon me to do in your place.[69]

The saint's advocacy is requested again elsewhere in the prayer, though this time his/her mediation is sought not between the abbot and his community, but before Christ Himself:

And you, O holy and blessed N., you are my advocate ('advocatus meus');
be my intercessor to God ('ad Deum intercessor').
I pray you, entreat him,
I beg you, beseech him.
Offer him my prayer,
and bring his favourable answer back to me.[70]

In the colophons, Mary also represents Frowin before Christ and advocates on his behalf in both this life and the afterlife.[71] Medieval gift giving was often transactional, and these books are no exception.[72] The verses on the illustrated frontispiece of the *Engelberg Bible*'s second volume (MS Engelberg 3) epitomise this: 'I [Frowin] offer you [Mary] a book, [will you] grant me absolution from my sins.' The salvation of Frowin's soul required not just the saint's singular intercession, however, but active – and

---

[69] 'Oratio', ed. Schmitt, 70; tr. Ward, 210.

[70] 'Oratio', ed. Schmitt, 69; tr. Ward, 209.

[71] Earthly protection is requested in nos. 5, 24, 28, and heavenly rewards in nos. 1, 2, 3, 4a, 4b, 6, 10, 16, 18, 19, 20, 21, 26, 27, 29, 30, and 36.

[72] L. Kjær, *The Medieval Gift and the Classical Tradition: Ideals and the Performance of Generosity in Medieval England, 1100–1300* (Cambridge: Cambridge University Press, 2019); G. Müller-Oberhäuser (ed.), *Book Gifts and Cultural Networks from the 14th to the 16th Century* (Münster: Rhema, 2019); C. Schleif, 'Gifts and Givers That Keep on Giving: Pictured Presentations in Early Medieval Manuscripts', in G. Donavin and A. Obermeier (eds.), *Romance and Rhetoric: Essays in Honour of Dhira B. Mahoney* (Turnhout: Brepols, 2010), pp. 51–74.

Figure 2 Frowin and Richene
Engelberg, Stiftsbibliothek, MS Cod. 5, fol. 1 r, reproduced with permission

continuous – participation by the books' prospective users too. The colophon in the *Explanatio Dominicae orationis*, Frowin's authorial composition, urges readers to recite a short prayer in his memory every time they use the book (no. 2), and even the books themselves are given a voice to encourage intercessory prayers on the readers' part (nos. 1, 21, and 30).

Perhaps the most instructive colophons for the purposes of this study are those that channel the voice of the books' scribe(s). The most striking, and the one that has attracted considerable scholarly attention, is that which accompanies the full-page miniature in the third tome of the *Engelberg Bible* (MS Engelberg 5; no. 6; Figure 2). Seated face to face underneath three painted arches are Frowin and his scribe, Richene, whom we met briefly in Chapter 2.[73] Placed between them on a writing desk is an open book with blank pages ready to be filled by Richene, who clutches a penknife with his raised right hand. The arrangement of hands is vital to the miniature's iconography: Frowin's left hand holds his abbatial staff/crozier, the source and symbol of his authority, and his right hand grants the licence to write by pointing across the desk to Richene with an extended index finger, the trajectory of which follows that of the desk's top edge. Without averting his gaze from Frowin, Richene receives the abbot's authority and continues the trajectory of his hand with the orientation of his penknife before redirecting it towards the book with the index finger of his left hand. As the verses written into the arches above Richene's head explain, his hand merely acts as an extension of Frowin's: 'As the scribe I did the writing, but my hand obeyed him ("manus . . . paruit ipsi").' As long as Frowin leads ('pracedit') and Richene obeys ('obedit'), abbot and scribe act as one person, and together they reap the eternal reward for the book's production and its provision to Engelberg's monastic community.

That this dynamic was not limited to the working relationship between Frowin and Richene, but also applied to other – indeed all – scribes in Engelberg's monastic scriptorium is shown by the fact that the same verses that accompany Richene's portrait also appear on the flyleaf of a copy of Augustine's *De sermone Domini in monte* (Engelberg, Stiftsbibliothek, MS Cod. 88; no. 27) penned by an anonymous monk-scribe, as well as by several

---

[73] Previous studies of this miniature and its iconography include Bonifazi, 'Miniaturen'; Steinmann, 'Frowin', 11 and 14; Feiss, 'Frowin', 91–2.

Figure 3 Frowin(?) as *auctor* alongside St Gregory
Cleveland, Museum of Art, Purchase from the J. H. Wade Fund 1955.74, fol.
[i] r, reproduced with permission

codices whose colophons credit Frowin as the one who ordered them to be written by virtue of his official authority.[74] As abbot, Frowin's superior authority in the production and endorsement of books entitled him to be recognised and commemorated alongside and above the scribes whose agency – and, save for Richene, whose identity – was subsumed by his own persona, and it even gave him quasi-authorial status alongside established authorities such as the Church Fathers. The colophon in the fourth part of the *Moralia in Iob* (Engelberg, Stiftsbibliothek, MS Cod. 23; no. 17) identifies Frowin, not Gregory, as the book's *author* ('auctor codicis huius'), whilst that in Engelberg's copy of the *Confessiones* (Engelberg, Stiftsbibliothek, MS Cod. 18; no. 12) stipulates that '[t]his book of Augustine is also the work of Frowin ("est opus ac Froewini")' because the former composed it and the latter had it copied ('scribendo notavit'). We should note that neither of these two codices was copied *manu propria* by Frowin. Meanwhile, the illustrated frontispiece of the first part of Engelberg's copy of Gregory's *Moralia* (Engelberg, Stiftsbibliothek, MS Cod. 20; now Cleveland, Museum of Art, Purchase from the J. H. Wade Fund 1955.74, fol. [i] r; Figure 3) depicts a tonsured figure who is seated opposite – and on eye level with – the text's author (who is identified by his episcopal regalia and rubric), their hands connected by an extended scroll, and the colophon of the companion volume (MS Engelberg 23) gives reason to suspect that this figure is meant to represent the book's *auctor*, Frowin. 'The one who was *rector* here was the *auctor* of this book,' riddles the colophon of a copy of Bede's Gospel homilies (Engelberg, Stiftsbibliothek, MS Cod. 47; no. 20) before disclosing this *rector*/*auctor*'s identity in the very next verse: Frowin.

What we have here is evidently not authorial publication as defined by Niskanen.[75] Except for the *Explanatio* (MS Einsiedeln 240), none of the books produced under Frowin contain works composed by him or his scribes, including those whose colophons style him as their *auctor* when in reality they are copies of works by the likes of Augustine, Gregory, and Bede.[76]

---

[74] For example, Einsiedeln, Stiftsbibliothek, MS Cod. 166 (413) (no. 1); Engelberg, Stiftsbibliothek, MS Cod. 15 (no. 10).

[75] See Introduction.

[76] The manuscript of Frowin's other authorial composition, *De laude* (MS Engelberg 46), might have been produced at St Blasien; Steinmann, 'Frowin', 26.

And unlike glossators and commentators claiming authorship alongside the scriptural and patristic *auctoritates* whose words they helped explain to contemporary readers,[77] Frowin had these texts copied from their exemplars without elucidation.[78] The same is true of Hugh of St Victor and Bernard of Clairvaux, whose works Frowin seems to have copied *manu propria*.[79] If we want to understand Frowin's role in the publication of these books, we need to consider the relationship between the medieval concepts of *auctor* and *auctoritas*.

On Bede's patristic reputation, see H. Mayr-Harting, 'Bede's Patristic Thinking As an Historian', in A. Scharer and G. Scheibelreiter (eds.), *Historiographie im frühen Mittelalter* (Vienna: Oldenbourg, 1994), pp. 367–74; B. M. Kaczynski, 'Bede's Commentaries on Luke and Mark and the Formation of a Patristic Canon', in S. Echard and G. R. Wieland (eds.), *Anglo-Latin and Its Heritage: Essays in Honour of A. G. Rigg on His 64th Birthday* (Turnhout: Brepols, 2001), pp. 17–26; T. Webber, 'Bede's *Historia Ecclesiastica* As a Source of Lections in Pre- and Post-Conquest England', in M. Brett and D. A. Woodman (eds.), *The Long Twelfth-Century View of the Anglo-Saxon Past* (Farnham: Ashgate, 2015), pp. 47–74.

[77] See Hamburger, *Birth*; Minnis, *Authorship*, 40–72; R. S. Sturges, 'Medieval Authorship and the Polyphonic Text: From Manuscripts Commentary to the Modern Novel', in T. J. Farrell (ed.), *Bakhtin and Medieval Voices* (Gainesville: University Press of Florida, 1996), pp. 122–37.

[78] As Steinmann notes, Engelberg's few glossed Bibles were all imported; Steinmann, 'Frowin', 21.

[79] Steinmann, 'Frowin', 20 and 27–8; besides the extant autographs of the *Explanatio* and *De laude*, manuscripts that Steinmann attributes to Frowin's hand are copies of Bernard's treatises *De consideratione* (Engelberg, Stiftsbibliothek, MS Cod. 139), *Sermones super Cantica Canticorum* (Engelberg, Stiftsbibliothek, MS Cod. 32), and *De gratia et libero arbitrio* (Engelberg, Stiftsbibliothek, MS Cod. 89), as well as a copy of Hugh's *De sacramentis fidei Chistianae* (Engelberg, Stiftsbibliothek, MS Cod. 90). Frowin seems to have limited his first-hand scribal activity to contemporary authors.

4 *Auctor* and *Auctoritas*

Part of the complication that arises from the colophons discussed in Chapter 2 has to do with the ambivalence of their terminology. This concerns, first and foremost, the term *auctor*. In classical Latin, *auctor* (from *augere*) denoted a maker, someone who produced something new and concrete – for example, a text – with creative agency, whilst *actor* (from *agere*) designated a maker in the wider sense, someone who through his/her actions enabled and facilitated a production process.[80] Whilst never completely distinct, these terms and their usage became blurred – and practically inverted – in medieval Latin, to the effect that *actor* was now increasingly applied to individuals engaged in original creation and composition, whereas *auctor* could describe those involved in facilitation, promotion, and, crucially, publication.[81] This ambivalence is not reflected in our modern usage(s) of the term *author*. In the Middle Ages, an *auctor* was not necessarily someone who composed or codified a work by putting pen to parchment (or wax tablet) personally, but could equally be someone who – like Frowin – lent his authority to an existing work; for example, by approving its dissemination and consumption amongst an audience such as the monastic community of Engelberg. By calling Frowin the *auctor* of the *Moralia*, the colophonist does not negate Gregory's authorship,[82] but rather adds to it the official authorisation of his own institutional superior. And when asking rhetorically for the *auctor* of Engelberg's copy of Bede's homilies, the answer given by the colophonist is the only one permissible in the

---

[80] Compare M.-D. Chenu, 'Auctor, Actor, Autor', *Archivum latinitatis medii aevi*, 3 (1927), 81–6 (p. 82); J.-D. Müller, '*Auctor–Actor–Author*: Einige Anmerkungen zum Verständnis vom Autor in lateinischen Schriften des frühen und hohen Mittelalters', in F. P. Ingold and W. Wunderlich (eds.), *Der Autor im Dialog: Beiträge zu Autorität und Autorschaft* (St Gall: UVK, 1995), pp. 17–31 (p. 18).

[81] Minnis, *Authorship*, 10: 'The term *auctor* denoted someone who was at once writer and authority ... An *auctor* "performed" the act of writing. He [or she] brought something into being [from Latin *agere*], caused it to 'grow' [from *augere*].'

[82] As noted by Minnis, *Authorship*, 11, '[i]t was regarded as a very drastic step to dispute an attribution and deprive a work of its *auctor*', which is not what we see in the colophons from Engelberg.

monastic hierarchy and chain of command: the *rector* – that is, the leader or governor; in other words, the abbot.

As abbot, Frowin's role as *auctor* was defined not by authorship, but by *auctoritas*. Like *auctor*, the term *auctoritas* requires some explanation.[83] In a literary context, *auctoritas* in medieval Latin designated the authority of a text or authorial oeuvre as well as citation from it.[84] Such authority was usually bestowed, rather than claimed, and to enjoy this privilege, an *auctor/opus* typically had to stand the test of time; that said, it seems a step too far to argue categorically that 'no "modern" writer could decently be called an *auctor* in a period in which men saw themselves as dwarfs standing on the shoulders of giants'.[85] And whilst it is true, generally speaking, that '[t]he recognition of a text as an *auctoritas* was considered the preserve of posterity',[86] this does not mean that works by contemporary authors could not be recognised as possessing authority, even if their *auctoritas* – unlike that of, say, Scripture or the Church Fathers, was not (or not yet) generally acknowledged or above suspicion. Frowin's own use of *auctoritates* provides a good case in point here. As we will recall, the two

---

[83] For an overview of the relevant scholarship, see K.-K. Alings, '*Auctoritas*: Semantische Studien zu einem Schlüsselbegriff des frühen Mittelalters', unpublished PhD dissertation, University of Cologne, 2019, pp. 7–15, noting that *auctoritas*, whilst a key concept (*Kernbegriff*) of medieval research, is very rarely defined in existing scholarship (p. 9).

[84] Müller, '*Auctor*', 18: 'Der Terminus *auctoritas* . . . bezeichnet das Zitat aus dem Werk eines *auctor*.' A similar definition is given by G. Berndt, 'Auctoritas', in *Lexikon des Mittelalters*, Studienausgabe, 9 vols. (Stuttgart: Metzler, 1999), vol. 1, p. 1190.

[85] See Minnis, *Authorship*, 12, concluding that 'it would seem that the only good *auctor* was a dead one'.

[86] l S. Niskanen, 'From Author to Authority: Anselm's Public Reputation and the Council of Bari (1098)', *Journal of Medieval History*, 49 (2023), 1–22 (p. 12). As Niskanen demonstrates in this study, Anselm of Le Bec/Canterbury was considered an *auctoritas* even amongst contemporaries, a recognition both reflected in and facilitated by the public citation of Anselm's writings at a major papal council. The importance of *auctoritas* in late antique/early medieval church councils and the codification of their acts is studied by T. Graumann, *The Acts of the Early Church Councils: Production and Character* (Oxford: Oxford University Press, 2021).

auctoritates cited most frequently in Frowin's own literary compositions (*Explanatio* and *De laude*) are Augustine and Gregory, whose works together account for nearly two thirds of the books Frowin provided for Engelberg's monastic library. Following closely in third place, however, we find a contemporary *auctor* and *auctoritas*: Bernhard of Clairvaux, whose three works *Sermones super Cantica Canticorum*, *De consideratione*, and *De gratia et libero arbitrio* Frowin even copied *manu propria*.[87] Bernard was not the only modern authority Frowin cited and had copied for the monastery's library. Others were Anselm of Le Bec/Canterbury (†1109), Hugh of St Victor (†1141), Honorius Augustodunensis (†1150/1), Richard of St Victor (†1173), and Werner (II) of St Blasien (†1178), all but one of whom were contemporaries – Werner even died in the same year as Frowin! – whose works Frowin considered authoritative and cutting-edge despite, or, perhaps, because of, their recent dates of composition.[88] And though their *auctoritas* was not of the same kind as Augustine's and Gregory's, it nevertheless came from a similar source, one that was different to the source from which Frowin derived his authority as abbot.

The source of Frowin's *auctoritas* as expressed in the colophons discussed in Chapter 3 was not primarily an authorial, but an official and institutional one. Rooted firmly in the monastic tradition, abbatial *auctoritas* – though second to none within the community – required communal recognition, which gave it a participatory and performative quality.[89] Unlike the received *auctoritas* of Scripture or the writings of the Church Fathers, that of the abbot, whilst

---

[87] See Chapter 3. [88] Feiss, 'Frowin', 196–204; Steinmann, 'Frowin', 20.

[89] P. Salmon, *L'abbé dans la tradition monastique: Contribution à l'histoire du caractère perpétuel des supérieurs religieux en Occident* (Paris: Sirey, 1992).

The participatory quality of *auctoritas* is also emphasised by J. Leemans and B. Meijns, 'Why Are Some Greater than Others? Actors and Factors Shaping the Authority of Persons from Antiquity to the Renaissance', in S. Boodts, J. Leemans, and B. Meijns (eds.), *Shaping Authority: How Did a Person Become an Authority in Antiquity, the Middle Ages and the Renaissance?* (Turnhout: Brepols, 2016), pp. 9–20 (p. 10). On *auctoritas* and tradition, compare K. Pollmann, 'Christianity and Authority in Late Antiquity: The Transformation of the Concept of *Auctoritas*', in C. Harrison, C. Humfress, and I. Sandwell (eds.), *Being Christian in Late Antiquity: A Festschrift for Gillian Clark* (Oxford: Oxford University Press, 2014), pp. 156–74 (pp. 166–7).

established in principle by normative texts such as the *Rule of St Benedict*,[90] needed regular reiteration and reactivation within the community's daily life and routine. As objects of communal usage, the manuscripts produced at Engelberg and inscribed with Frowin's name were active vehicles for this collective performance and perpetuation of abbatial *auctoritas*. But what role did this *auctoritas* play in the books' release and distribution?

As should be clear by now, we are dealing with a mode of production, licensing, release, and distribution that must be distinguished from authorial publishing as defined by Niskanen and others, one that aligns more closely, if not perfectly, with Riddy's official publishing.[91] As noted already, Riddy primarily relates this mode of publication to new literary compositions released for the first time, and more specifically still to religious writings licensed by an ecclesiastical authority.[92] Whilst most books discussed in this study fit the second category (besides Frowin's authorial works), none belongs in the first. What is more, for Riddy, the main differentiating factor between authorial and official publication is not whether the books contain authorial works (they all do), but whether the authority responsible for their release and dissemination is the author him-/herself or a third party acting on his/her behalf, either directly or via intermediaries and interlocutors. Both scenarios require the author(s) to be alive, to be present, and to take an active part in the process. As we saw, however, this was evidently not the case with most books in Engelberg's monastic library. Does that mean, though, that the process through which these books were licensed, released, and authorised to enter the realm of communal consumption cannot be viewed as publishing?

How we answer this question hinges on two factors: first, how we define (a) public, and, second, how central we consider the author's role in the publication process. Beginning with the former, there is little reason to deny monastic communities the ability to act in a public capacity. As observed by Jaakko Tahkokallio, many works produced in medieval monasteries (perhaps the majority) were not destined and designed for an 'open literary

---

[90] A. de Vogüé, *Community and Abbot in the Rule of Saint Benedict* (Kalamazoo, MI: Cistercian Publications, 1979).

[91] See Introduction.   [92] Riddy, '"Publication"', 30.

public sphere',[93] but this does not mean that those confined (accidentally or by design) to institutional spheres did not undergo similar processes of licensing and authorisation, nor does it mean that they should be considered unpublished. The following example may illustrate this. In an oft-quoted passage from his chronicle, Frowin's contemporary, Gervase of Canterbury, styles himself as writing not for a general readership, but for his monastic community of Canterbury Cathedral Priory ('non bibliotecae publicae sed tibi, mi frater Thoma, et nostra familiolae pauperculae scribo') – a statement which may be (and has been) taken to suggest that monastic writers usually expected their works to remain confidential, and that internal release and confinement to the community did not constitute acts of publication.[94] This is unconvincing, however. Once a work was licensed and an authorised copy – often the authorial/presentation copy itself – deposited in the monastery's library, there was only so much an author could do to control and constrain its subsequent use and distribution within and without the institution.[95] This is true especially, but by no means exclusively, of well-connected monasteries that regularly engaged in book

---

[93] Tahkokallio, *Canon*, 2. See also J. Tahkokallio, 'Rewriting English History for a High-Medieval Republic of Letters: Henry of Huntingdon, William of Malmesbury, and the Renaissance of the Twelfth Century', in E. Winkler and C. Lewis (eds.), *Rewriting History in the Central Middle Ages, 900–1300* (Turnhout: Brepols, 2022), pp. 169–94.

[94] *The Historical Works of Gervase of Canterbury*, ed. W. Stubbs, 2 vols. (London: Longman, 1979–80; repr. Cambridge: Cambridge University Press, 2012), vol. 1, p. 89; Tahkokallio, *Canon*, 71. Similar arguments have also been made about the work of Gervase's predecessor, Eadmer; for discussion and rebuttal of the latter, see Pohl and Tether, 'Eadmer'. On medieval notions of the *bibliotheca publica*, again with specific reference to and detailed discussion of Gervase's statement, see J. Kujawiński, 'Between the Ancient Model and Its Humanistic Revival: The Notion of *Bibliotheca Publica* in the Middle Ages', in M. Delimata-Proch, J. Kujawiński, and A. Krawiec (eds.), Totius mundi philohistor: *Studia Georgio Strzelczyk octuagenario oblata* (Poznan: Adam Mickiewicz University, 2021), pp. 415–29 (pp. 415–18).

[95] Some eleventh- and twelfth-century authors even struggled, and failed, to control the distribution of their works in draft form; for a pertinent example, see Sharpe, 'Anselm', passim.

exchanges and interlibrary loans, often over considerable distances.[96] And though Engelberg's library network did not rival Canterbury's in the twelfth century, it was closely linked – and shared mutual library access – with at least two (and likely more) other communities, chief amongst them Muri and St Blasien.[97]

At Engelberg and elsewhere, there was an expectation that access to books would generally be granted to affiliated houses (and vice versa) unless there were good reasons not to comply with a specific request – for example, if the book in question was considered indispensable or too precious/fragile to travel, if its text was found defective or corrupted to such a degree that producing further copies posed a reputational risk to the lender and/or borrower, or if the borrowing party had a track record of not returning books in good time. Evidence of this survives from across medieval Europe in the shape of personal and official correspondence by monastic superiors requesting shared library access and book-borrowing rights from their abbatial peers. When Odilo, abbot of La Croix-Saint-Leufroy, asked for a book from the monastic library of Le Bec-Hellouin in the early 1070s, he was told by its prior, Anselm (the later archbishop of Canterbury), that 'we would gladly comply with your request and send you the book . . ., if only we had it here';[98] unfortunately, the book in question had already been loaned to the abbey of Saint-Étienne de Caen at the request of its abbot, William I, to produce two copies, one for Caen and the other, copied at the request of Archbishop Lanfranc, for Canterbury

---

[96] On monastic interlibrary-loan networks, see the recent discussion in Pohl, *Abbatial Authority*.

[97] On Canterbury's twelfth-century library, see M. R. James, *The Ancient Libraries of Canterbury and Dover* (Cambridge: Cambridge University Press, 1903); R. Eales and R. Sharpe (eds.), *Canterbury and the Norman Conquest: Churches, Saints, and Scholars, 1066–1109* (London: Hambledon, 1995). For a case study, see B. Pohl, 'Who Wrote Paris, BnF, Latin 2342? The Identity of the *Anonymus Beccensis* Revisited', in C. Denoël and F. Siri (eds.), *France et Angleterre: Manuscrits médiévaux entre 700 et 1200* (Turnhout: Brepols, 2020), pp. 153–89.

[98] *Letters of Anselm, Archbishop of Canterbury, Vol. 1: The Bec Letters*, ed./tr. S. Niskanen (Oxford: Clarendon, 2019), pp. 384–7 (i.312); also compare ibid., 59–65 and 380–3 (i.19 and i.130).

Cathedral Priory, the future home of Gervase (see earlier in this chapter). However, Anselm hastens to reassure Abbot Odilo that 'as soon as we get the book back, we will gladly lend it . . . according to your wish'.[99] A centre of book production and collection whose reputation – and institutional network – radiated far beyond Normandy, Le Bec's books were in high demand,[100] and their timely return was of the essence to help accommodate future requests. Having nearly caused a diplomatic incident by prompting Caen's prior and abbot to return some long-overdue volumes, Anselm quickly issued an apologetic reassurance that they could hold on to the books for as long as they were needed, adding that, with his abbot's authorisation, 'we will unreservedly send you whichever books . . . on your demand, for our *mutual* benefit'.[101]

Contemporary monastic libraries facing similar levels of demand include that at Tegernsee, where the abbot's *secretarius*, a monk called Fromund, politely declined an external request to lend out the community's annotated two-volume copy of Boethius because one volume was a confined 'desk copy' and the other on loan to Augsburg along with another book from Tegernsee's library in exchange for two of their books.[102] As soon as the book is back at Tegernsee, Fromund assures

---

[99] *Letters*, ed./tr. Niskanen, 386–7.

[100] Le Bec's sometime monk and prior, Robert of Torigni, famously commissioned a detailed inventory of its library after his abbatial appointment at Mont-Saint-Michel that survives on the flyleaves of his *Chronica* ('Tituli librorum Beccensis almarii'; Avranches, Bibliothèquemunicipale, MS 159, fols. 2 r–3 r), presumably so he could continue to borrow its books after his departure in 1154; edited most recently by L. Cleaver, 'The Monastic Library at Le Bec', in B. Pohl and L. L. Gathagan (eds.), *A Companion to the Abbey of Le Bec in the Central Middle Ages (11th–13th Centuries)* (Leiden: Brill, 2017), pp. 171–205 (pp. 195–205). See also B. Pohl, '*Abbas qui et scriptor?* The Handwriting of Robert of Torigni and His Scribal Activity As Abbot of Mont-Saint-Michel (1154–1186)', *Traditio*, 69 (2014), 45–86 (p. 51).

[101] *Letters*, ed./tr. Niskanen, 32–7 (i.10); my emphasis.

[102] Edited in *Die Tegernseer Briefsammlung (Froumund)*, ed. K. Strecker (Berlin: Weidmann, 1925), p. 18 (no. 17). There is also another letter (written anonymously) in the Tegernsee corpus that requests the loan of several volumes; *Die*

his correspondent, the request to borrow it next will be accommodated as a matter of course. As these and similar cases discussed in detail elsewhere make clear, the mutual lending and borrowing of books was common practice amongst monastic communities of the eleventh and twelfth centuries, and the default setting was that access would be granted liberally, even if this involved a deposit, pledge, or similar kind of reassurance to minimise the risk of late return and discourage alienation or theft.[103] The statutes issued at the Council of Paris in 1212 even explicitly forbade monasteries and their superiors to refuse loaning their books to others who needed them with the exception of certain books retained in-house for the monks' daily work ('in domo ad opus fratrum retineantur'). All other books were to be made available freely upon request provided that doing so would cause no loss or damage to the lending community – a risk that should be determined by its abbot's own judgement ('secundum providentiam abbatis').[104]

In the face of such testimony, any categoric reservation about referring to monastic book production and exchange as a form of publishing seems unjustified. On the contrary, the picture that emerges with increasing clarity is one of relatively free and open access to books facilitated by large trans-institutional networks and publishing communities. Even if we are hesitant to apply the term to the members of a single monastic community, there can be little doubt that collectively these networks and communities constituted a *public*. In fact, the common practice of interlibrary loans casts some doubt on whether the number and distribution of copies are reliable indicators of publication in a monastic context. If one monastery's copy could be borrowed or read in situ by visitors, then the absence of further physical copies in another monastery does not have to indicate that a work was unknown there, and even confinement to a single monastic library did not have to prevent a book from

Tegernseer Briefsammlung des 12: Jahrhunderts, ed. H. Plechl and W. Bergmann (Hanover: Hahn, 2002), pp. 260–1 (no. 230).

[103] See the discussion in Pohl, *Abbatial Authority*.

[104] 'Statutorum concilii Parisiensis pars secunda: Ad viros regulares', in G. D. Mansi (ed.), *Sacrorum conciliorum nova et amplissima collectio*, 31 vols. (Venice: Zatta, 1758–98), vol. 22, p. 832.

obtaining both wider reception and published status. Put more polemically still, the holdings of a monastery's domestic library may well be an altogether insufficient and inaccurate indicator of the literary horizon and collective 'knowledge bank' of its inhabitants. Which texts were available to and considered public knowledge by a monastic readership may thus have depended much less on individual in-house collections than on larger library networks and the sum of titles accessible through them. Medieval monasticism was, after all, a communal experience supported by shared knowledge and confraternity, and books were the primary vehicles of this mutual knowledge exchange.

This brings us back to our second consideration, the author's role in the publishing process. As noted earlier in this Element and demonstrated at length elsewhere, medieval authors exercised some control in the release and dissemination of their works.[105] Their agency had its limits, however, and monastic book production was governed by institutional rather than individual or authorial *auctoritas*. The following example is instructive. In his discussion of the *Gesta regum Anglorum* written by William of Malmesbury for Matilda, queen consort of England (1100–18), Tahkokallio identifies the beginning of the publication process as the very moment at which William's monastery presented the finished work to Empress Matilda, the late patroness' daughter, and her uncle, King David I of Scotland, in 1125.[106] Were it not for the significant fact that Malmesbury was going through an abbatial interregnum at the time, however – following the death of Abbot Eadwulf in 1118, the community was governed by the bishop of Salisbury until 1139/40 – we usually would expect the *auctoritas abbatis*, not the *auctoritas regia*, to

---

[105] For the period under consideration in this Element, I again refer the reader to the case studies by Niskanen, 'Authorial Publication'; Niskanen, 'Authorial Culture'; Tahkokallio, *Canon*; and Sharpe, 'Anselm'.

[106] Tahkokallio, *Canon*, 21–3. The letters accompanying the presentation copy are written not in William's voice, but by the entire community; *William of Malmesbury: Gesta regum Anglorum – The History of the English Kings*, ed./tr. R. A. B. Mynors, R. M. Thomson, and M. Winterbottom, 2 vols. (Oxford: Clarendon, 1998–9), vol. 1, pp. 2–5 (to David) and 6–9 (to Matilda); E. Könsgen, 'Zwei unbekannte Briefe zu den *Gesta regum Anglorum* des Wilhelm von Malmesbury', *Deutsches Archiv für Erforschung des Mittelalters*, 31 (1975), 204–14 (pp. 211–14).

commence the process of publication. That the work was released immediately to Matilda (via David) during this protracted absence of abbatial leadership is an exception that proves the rule.[107] Internal authorisation and external dissemination were two distinct yet intrinsically related aspects of the monastic publication process, and the former typically preceded the latter. Patrons outside the monastery were important and influential agents in this process whose help and endorsement could be instrumental for a work's external distribution and wider reception, but within the community their authority – just like everyone else's – was subordinate to the monastic superior's.

The reason books – authorial and non-authorial – produced within monasteries were subject to abbatial authorisation and licensing is twofold. On the one hand, it reflects the basic principle – set out in the *Rule of St Benedict* and reiterated in monastic customaries across Europe – that no writing should take place, no writing tools and bookmaking materials be distributed, and no scribal work be assigned without the abbot's licence and approval. It was the abbot's responsibility to ensure, usually via delegated officials, that the monks were provided with everything they needed to go about their work, and by supplying them with tools, materials, and, crucially, time for writing, he assumed responsibility for the products of their labour. When Richene and his fellow scribes refer to their hands as extensions of Frowin's (nos. 6 and 27), they are not just presenting themselves as writing with their abbot's authority, but also passing on responsibility for their work to him. Indeed, it was the abbot who would have to stand before God on judgement day and answer for the scribes' work. And when Engelberg's colophonist asks for equal reward for the one who leads (the abbot) and the one who obeys (the scribe), this therefore

---

[107] In fact, the letter to David asks him to add his authority ('auctoritas') because his sister had left the community without an abbot ('quod absque pastore gregem ecclesiae nostrae liquerit'); *Gesta*, ed./tr. Mynors, Thomson, and Winterbottom, 4–5. A similar point is made in the letter to Matilda (ibid., 6–7). Another contemporary exception is Eadmer of Canterbury, who seems to have timed the publication of his *Historia novorum in Anglia* to fall within a vacancy between the tenures of his institutional superiors; Pohl and Tether, 'Eadmer'.

serves at once as an avowal of monastic obedience and a spiritual insurance policy. Again, Anselm's prayer discussed in Chapter 3 provides us with a helpful parallel and contextualisation:

> But you, O apostle of God,
> you can raise up me [the abbot] and them [the monks].
> Carry me and them, excuse me and them!
> Help us all, rule, and protect us all,
> so that I may rejoice in their salvation with me
> ('ut et ego gaudens de illorum salute mecum'),
> and they in mine with them ('et illi de mea secum').[108]

On the other hand, abbatial authorisation was a means of quality control aimed at protecting the community and its reputation. Internally, it confirmed that a book was deemed safe for consumption by the community's members. This was important not just for new compositions whose contents had to be confirmed as suitable for a monastic readership, but equally for new copies of existing works, including – and especially – texts that were considered authoritative and canonical in the monastic context. As we saw in Chapter 3, most books produced during Frowin's abbacy fell into this latter category by providing Engelberg's monks with copies of Scripture and writings by established *auctoritates* like Bede, Gregory, and, first and foremost, Augustine. As abbot, Frowin's crucial role and responsibility in the release and dissemination of these volumes was not to establish whether they were suitable in principle for inclusion in the monastic library – the Bible's authority was above suspicion, and the same was true of most patristic authors – but to corroborate that they had been copied faithfully, were free of textual errors and corruptions, and could thus be used safely by the monks.

That corrupted copies of authoritative books were seen as a risk to a community's well-being is shown by evidence of monastic superiors expressing serious concerns about the presence of deficient copies in their abbeys' libraries, with some going to great lengths to source replacements as a matter of priority and urgency. A good example of this can be found in the

---

[108] 'Oratio', ed. Schmitt, 70; tr. Ward, 211.

correspondence of Anselm, whom we have met several times already. Writing to a monk of Le Bec named Maurice who had accompanied Lanfranc to Canterbury following the latter's archiepiscopal appointment and sojourned at the Cathedral Priory for several years, Anselm asks Maurice to send, with Lanfranc's approval, Canterbury's library copy of Bede's *De temporibus* to Le Bec because the copy kept there is in urgent need of correction ('propter ea quae in nostro scis esse corrigenda').[109] Anselm further asks Maurice to copy and send to Le Bec various other volumes from Canterbury's famously well-stocked library, explicitly urging him that 'whatever you complete should, after it has been most meticulously corrected, deserve to be regarded as perfect. For ... I prefer an intact fraction to a corrupt whole'.[110] As Le Bec's long-serving prior acting and writing on behalf of the ageing abbot, Herluin, whom he would succeed just a few years later, Anselm's concern about reliable copies clearly had the entire monastic community in mind. This included the seconded Maurice, whom Anselm cautions in another letter to shun books that contained anything scandalous or corruptive.[111]

Like Anselm at Le Bec, Frowin at Engelberg played an active part in copying library books and ensuring their integrity by occasionally correcting the work of his scribes *manu propria* and even copying some volumes in their entirety.[112] However, even books in whose production Frowin had no demonstrable first-hand involvement – which constitute the majority of the extant corpus – bear the hallmark of his abbatial *auctoritas* in the shape of the colophons discussed in Chapter 3 and collated in the Appendix. Inscribing books with Frowin's name served a dual purpose: internally, it acted as confirmation that the books had been produced with abbatial licence and approved for use by the community's members; externally, it provided users with access to Engelberg's library with assurance that the books contained

---

[109] *Letters*, ed./tr. Niskanen, 104–7 (i.34) (pp. 106–7). On Anselm and Maurice, see Pohl, '*Anonymus Beccensis*', passim.

[110] *Letters*, ed./tr. Niskanen, 146–9 (i.51): '[U]t quicquid feceris, studiosissima exquisitione correctum dignum sit dici perfectum. Malo enim in ignota inusitataque scriptura partem integram ueritate quam totum corruptum falsitate' (ibid., 146).

[111] *Letters*, ed./tr. Niskanen, 159–61 (i.55). [112] Steinmann, 'Frowin', 27–8.

authorised copies whose reliability had been ascertained, at the same time as safeguarding against their unauthorised removal of theft by asserting institutional ownership.[113] In both cases, the colophons marked the books as officially published and safe for consumption and copying, with Frowin and the abbey's patroness, the Virgin Mary, acting as the licensing authorities.

One question left to raise is whether the use of colophons for licensing the non-authorial production, release, and dissemination of manuscripts at Engelberg was Frowin's own invention or a practice he had inherited from his predecessors. As we saw in Chapter 2, his immediate precursors at Engelberg – the three *ababbates* Luitfried, Welfo, and Hesso – provided few (if any) books to the community over the course of their ill-remembered tenures, whereas Adelhelm's initial book acquisition policy had relied predominantly on the import of existing volumes from Muri, rather than on in-house production. In the absence of domestic precedents, there is also the possibility that Frowin imported this practice from elsewhere, most likely perhaps from his former home of St Blasien. This possibility finds support in the survival of at least one manuscript from St Blasien produced prior to Frowin's abbacy with a colophon dedicated to Abbot Uto (1086–1108), though the existence of similar inscriptions at other contemporary monasteries – albeit never used with the same frequency and variety as at Engelberg – prevents a definite conclusion.[114] On balance, therefore, it seems most plausible that Frowin adopted and/or adapted, rather than invented, the use of colophons as markers of abbatial *auctoritas* in the monastic publication of books. What we do know, meanwhile, is that this practice continued under Frowin's successors, even if not with the same level of consistency. Of the books made domestically under Berchtold and Henry I, some eleven survive with equivalent inscriptions (nine for

---

[113] See Engelberg, Stiftsbibliothek, MS Cod. 76, fol. 1 r (no. 25). Contrary to the interpretations in previous scholarship, however, this assertation of ownership constituted a secondary, not a primary function of the colophons; Steinmann, 'Frowin', 13; Feiss, 'Frowin', 85.

[114] Uto's colophon survives in St Paul in Kärnten, Stiftsbibliothek, MS 18/1; printed in Steinmann, 'Frowin', 14. For further examples, see *Colophons*, ed. Bénédictins de Bouveret, passim.

Berchtold and two for Henry), some of which even repeat/reuse the wording of Frowin's colophons verbatim (see Appendix, b and c). Berchtold and Henry's abbacies marked a period of increased scribal and artistic productivity at Engelberg that was not sustained by their thirteenth- and fourteenth-century successors, none of whom has left us with more than a single colophon in his name (ibid., d–g).[115]

Exploring the reasons for this gradual decline in the use of colophons at Engelberg lies outside the scope of this Element, but it may well reflect a relative decrease in domestic book production over time or even the eventual disappearance of the domestic scriptorium after a highly prolific period under three generations of abbots whose combined tenures spanned nearly a century. It was during Frowin's abbacy, however, that the monastic library experienced its single most significant and transformative expansion, elevating it from a basic stock of mostly liturgical books produced exter- nally and assembled by Adelhelm to a rich collection of *auctoritates* copied by domestic scribes to support teaching, study, and even new composition, with some still being preserved in situ. Encountered by various readers over the centuries, their colophons continue to promote and sustain the *auctoritas* of Frowin and his twelfth-century successors as monastic publishers both at Engelberg and beyond.

---

[115] Compare Bruckner (ed.), *Scriptoria*, 46–61; Feiss, 'Frowin', 82–3.

5 Conclusion

This Element has engaged with and responded to recent research into medieval publishing with a case study of some forty or so books produced at the Benedictine monastery of Engelberg during the tenure – and with the *auctoritas* – of its twelfth-century abbot, Frowin (1143–78). The evidence studied and interpreted here is not new, of course. The books made under Frowin are well known to medievalists and have been freely accessible in digital, iiiF-compliant format for more than a decade. Their colophons too have received some attention, though their function has been considered mainly as a means of ascertaining institutional book ownership. Indeed, one of the colophons' main uses in scholarship has been to help date and localise individual manuscripts, including those no longer preserved at Engelberg. Where contextual interpretations have been offered, they have typically focused on the colophons' symbolic and spiritual significance in the com- memoration of Frowin's person and the veneration of Mary, the commu- nity's patron saint. Revisiting and recontextualising these colophons in the light of monastic publication practices has revealed a new and important dimension of their design and functionality, one that – as I hope to have shown – is instrumental to our understanding of manuscript production, licensing, release, and distribution both at Engelberg and elsewhere in twelfth-century Europe.

It should be restated that the arguments presented in this Element are built on the premise that the processes by which medieval manuscript books were produced, licensed, released, and disseminated can be thought of and referred to as a form of *publishing* – a premise supported by a fast-growing tradition of scholarship including Elements published in the same Gathering as this one. As noted in the Introduction/Chapter 1, most attention so far has been paid to authorial modes of publication that involve new literary compositions released and disseminated by the author him-/herself or a third party acting on their behalf. This Element has taken a rather different approach by focusing on the production, licensing, release, and internal/external dissemi- nation of manuscripts that contain copies of existing texts, including those that were considered authoritative (*auctoritates*) and canonical such as the Bible or the writings of the Church Fathers. Most of the books surviving from

Engelberg's twelfth-century library belong in this category, which begs the question who authorised their copying, release, and distribution in the author's absence, often centuries after their original composition. As I have argued here, the answer to this question can be found in the role of the monastic superior: Frowin. As discussed in Chapter 2, Frowin was the first abbot of Engelberg whose book provision relied on domestic production serviced by an internal scribal workshop or scriptorium – a term that, as we saw, should be used with caution given the likely scale of the operation. Under Frowin's leadership, the basic stock of books for the liturgy and monastic observance assembled by his abbatial predecessors from external supply channels was transformed into a library suitable for study and teaching, the contents of which were mostly copied in-house from exemplars borrowed from the libraries of other monasteries with whom Engelberg was affiliated and connected via interlibrary-loan networks.

As abbot, Frowin not only had to authorise the provision of writing materials, their distribution, and the assignment of all scribal work within the community in keeping with the expectations expressed in monastic rules and customaries such as those discussed in Chapter 3, but he also assumed ex officio responsibility for all books produced with his abbatial licence. In line with twelfth-century trends, he furnished Engelberg's library with major works by Augustine, Gregory, and Bede, but he also commissioned copies of more recent and contemporary authors such as Anselm of Canterbury, Bernard of Clairvaux, and others whose *auctoritas* – unlike that of the Church Fathers and other universally acknowledged *auctoritates* – had yet to be established beyond doubt, and whose release to a monastic readership therefore demanded the abbot's authorisation. Even copies of Scripture and patristic works required some quality control before being deposited in monastic libraries, if only to ensure that they had been copied faithfully and were free from content that could confuse or, worse still, mislead impressionable or unmindful readers. As we saw in Chapter 4, monastic superiors regularly used their official *auctoritas* to commission and authorise the production, use, and circulation of books within their communities, at the same time as safeguarding their reputation externally. Frowin is no exception, and the verses that adorn no fewer than 90 per cent of the extant volumes produced at Engelberg during his abbacy are vivid testimony to the creativity with which this abbatial *auctoritas* was exercised, inscribed, and, on occasion, even illustrated on the manuscript page.

This Element's contribution to knowledge is twofold: on the one hand, it provides an in-depth study of scribal colophons in the context of twelfth-century monastic book production, one that offers a fresh and so far largely unexplored perspective on the history and cultural heritage of a medieval monastery whose tradition lives on today. On the other hand, it also marks an intervention in the field of premodern publishing studies by directing our view to a mode of publication that has received only limited attention in scholarship, at the same time as entering into dialogue with current research published in similarly accessible formats by Niskanen, Tahkokallio, and others. To be clear, my intention here is not to contest their approaches and interpretations, not even where they rely on similar kinds of evidence, but rather to enrich and diversify existing discourse by drawing specific attention to the crucial authority and agency of institutional superiors in processes of monastic book production, publication, and medieval manuscript culture. If medieval monasteries were indeed 'the earliest publishing houses' as asserted by de Hamel, then Abbot Frowin was Engelberg's foremost publisher. His case will, I hope, prove a useful impulse for continuing this fruitful and important conversation.

Appendix
Colophons in Manuscripts from Engelberg

Editorial note: in transcribing the colophons, I have added certain punctuation – for example, to indicate scansion – and normalised variant letters such as i/j, u/v, uu/w, and so forth. I have retained majuscules where they appear in the manuscripts and *e caudata* (ę) in place of the diphthong ae/æ. The English translations aim to strike a balance between literal translation and easy readability, with semantic clarifications added in square brackets. Colophons produced after Frowin's abbacy remain untranslated but are included in transcription for the sake of comparison and completeness.

a) Frowin (1143–78) [36 colophons]

1. Einsiedeln, Stiftsbibliothek, MS Cod. 166 (413)
   'Huic qui me iussit | scribi, pax, uita, salus sit; // Abraheque sinus; | abbas fuit ille FRO[W]INUS.' (p. 1)
   ('May peace, life, and prosperity be to him who ordered me to be written, and [may he be in] Abraham's bosom; he was Abbot FROWIN.')

2. Einsiedeln, Stiftsbibliothek, MS Cod. 240 (641)
   'Hoc precor, hoc hortor, | dic devota prece lector, // felix FROWINUS, | quod sit, agat Dominus; // ut verum lumen | cęleste daret sibi numen. // Huius scripta libri, | nam studuit fieri.' (p. 468)

('This I pray, this I urge, declare with devout prayer, O reader: "May the Lord make FROWIN blessed, so that the Divine will may grant him the true heavenly light"; for he strove for the writing of this book to be undertaken.')

3. Einsiedeln, Stiftsbibliothek, MS Cod. 360 (177)

'[H]ac de scriptura, | FROWINE, fuit tibi cura. // [Fr]atribus ut fieret, | mercesque tibi remaneret.' (fol. 1 r)

('You, Frowin, took care of these writings so that they may be [available] for the brothers, and the reward may remain with you.')

4. Engelberg, Stiftsbibliothek, MS Cod. 3

(a) "O genitrix Christi, | pax mundi, gloria coeli, // Dono tibi librum, | mi(c)hi da veniam vitiorum.' (fol. 1 v)

('O Mother of Christ, peace of the world, glory of heaven; I offer you a book, grant me absolution from [my] sins.')

(b) 'Conferat iste liber, | quod sis a crimine liber // O FROWIN, Christi |
    quem laudibus attribuisti.' (fol. 2 r)

('May this book that you have assigned to the glory of Christ confer that
    you shall be free from sin, O FROWIN.')

5. Engelberg, Stiftsbibliothek, MS Cod. 4[1]

    'Ista tibi dona | Genitrix et Virgo patrona. // Frowinum dantem |
    serves apud omnitonantem.' (fol. 1 v)

    'O Mother and Virgin patroness, protect before God [literally: All-
    Thunderer] Frowin, the giver of these gifts to you.')

---

[1] Possibly inserted after Frowin's death; see Steinmann, 'Frowin', 12, n. 21.

6. Engelberg, Stiftsbibliothek, MS Cod. 5

'Cur aut unde minus | habet a mercede Frowinus? // Cum scriptor scripsi, | manus autem paruit ipsi. // Dum bene praecedit hic, | dum catus alter obedit // Merces amborum | florebit in arce polorum.' (fol. 1 r)

('Why and for what reason should Frowin have less of the reward [than I]? As the scribe I did the writing, but my hand obeyed him. For as long as this one [= Frowin] leads well and the other [= the scribe] obeys prudently, the reward of both will blossom in the heavenly citadel.')

7. Engelberg, Stiftsbibliothek, MS Cod. 9

'Hoc pie Christe datum | Berctoldi [formerly: Frowini] sit tibi gratum.' (fol. 11 r)

('May this gift by Berchtold [formerly: Frowin] be pleasing to you, O Holy Christ.')

8. Engelberg, Stiftsbibliothek, MS Cod. 12

'Psalmorum lumen | noscas hoc esse volumen. // Institit id fieri | FROWI(N) pro lumine veri.' (fol. 1 r)

('Do know this book carries the light of [the] Psalms. Frowin set about to have it made for the light of truth.')

9. Engelberg, Stiftsbibliothek, MS Cod. 13
   'O Frowine pater, | fugiat te spiritus ater. // Quod David condit, | per te liber hic quia pandit.' (fol. 1 r)
   ('O Father Frowin, may the deadly spirit shun you, for thanks to you this book explains what David writes.')

10. Engelberg, Stiftsbibliothek, MS Cod. 15
    'FROWINO lumen | coeli ferat hocce VOLUMEN. // Nam PERSCRIPSIT IDEM | PRECIPIENDO QUIDEM.') (fol. 1 r)
    ('May this book bring Frowin the heavenly light. For he wrote and indeed ordered it.')

11. Engelberg, Stiftsbibliothek, MS Cod. 16
    'Hunc Augustini | librum studiosa Frowini // Sancta Maria tibi | fecit devotio scribi.' (fol. 1 r)

('The zealous devotion of Frowin had this book of Augustine written
for you, Holy [Virgin] Mary.')

12. Engelberg, Stiftsbibliothek, MS Cod. 18
    'Hic AUGUSTINI | liber est opus ac Froewini, // Alter dictavit, |
    alter scribendo NOTAVIT.' (fol. 1 r)
    ('This book of Augustine is also the work of Frowin. One composed
    [it], and the other designated it to be copied.')

13. Engelberg, Stiftsbibliothek, MS Cod. 19
    'Hac in scriptura | Frowine patet tua cura. // Hanc vigilis mentis, |
    quia scripsisti documentis.' (fol. 4 r)
    ('In this writing your zeal lies open, Frowin, for you wrote it as proof
    of a vigilant mind.')

14. Cleveland, Museum of Art, Purchase from the J. H. Wade Fund
    1955.74, fol. [i] v (formerly Engelberg, Stiftsbibliothek, MS Cod. 20)
    'Hunc famulis Christi | FROWINE librum tribuisti // Ut Christo
    revocet | quos liber iste docet.' (fol. †1 v)
    ('You, Frowin, presented this book to the servants of Christ, so
    that it would make those whom this very book teaches recall
    Christ.')

15. Engelberg, Stiftsbibliothek, MS Cod. 21

    'Librum presentem | qui no(ve)rit pascere mentem // FROWINI studia | cumulant tibi sancta MARIA.' (fol. 1 r)

    ('It was for you, Holy [Virgin] Mary, that the efforts of Frowin produced the present book, which can nurture the mind.')

16. Engelberg, Stiftsbibliothek, MS Cod. 22

    'Det lumen verum | FROWIN tibi lux pia rerum // Dogma per hoc Christi | secreta quod [he]edocuisti.' (fol. 1 r)

    ('May the holy light give you the true light, Frowin, for you have taught the hidden doctrine of things related to Christ.')

17. Engelberg, Stiftsbibliothek, MS Cod. 23

    'Codex finitur | quo Iob sapiens aperitur. // Abbas FROWINUS | fuit auctor codicis HUIUS.' (fol. 123 v)

('The book by which the wise Job is explained closes here. Abbot Frowin was the author of this book.')

18. Engelberg, Stiftsbibliothek, MS Cod. 32

'Pectoris ob lumen, | pater hoc FROWINE volumen // fecisti fieri; | sit talio, notio veri.' (fol. 3 r)

('You, Father Frowin, had this book made for the enlightenment of the soul. May the reward be the understanding of truth.')

19. Engelberg, Stiftsbibliothek, MS Cod. 46

'Has FROWIN cartas, | electo dogmate fartas, // fecit conscribi. | Fac bene Christe sibi.' (fol. 1 r)

('Frowin had these pages, full of excellent doctrine, copied. Do right by him, O Christ!')

20. Engelberg, Stiftsbibliothek, MS Cod. 47

'Qui fuit hic rector, | fuit huius codicis auctor. // Frowin, ob quod ei | sit favor opto Dei.' (fol. 1 r)

('The one who was leader here was the author of this book. Frowin, and for that I wish him the Lord's favour.')

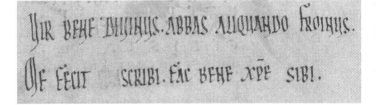

21. Engelberg, Stiftsbibliothek, MS Cod. 48
    'VIR BENE DIVINUS | ABBAS ALIQUANDO FRO[W]INUS //
    ME FECIT CONSCRIBI. | FAC BENE CHRISTE SIBI.' (fol. 1 r)
    ('The most religious man and sometime abbot Frowin had me written
    [down]. Do right by him, O Christ!')

22. Engelberg, Stiftsbibliothek, MS Cod. 49
    'Quod vetus occultat | lex, hoc liber hic manifestat; // quare Frowinus
    | conscripsit eum studiosus.' (fol. 1 r)
    ('What the ancient law conceals this book here reveals, wherefore
    Frowin zealously committed it to writing.')

23. Engelberg, Stiftsbibliothek, MS Cod. 64
    'Omnibus iste bonis | liber placet exameronis, // quem matri Christi,
    | pater o Frowine dedisti.' (fol. 1 r)

('This book of the Hexameron that you, Father Frowin, have given to
the Mother of Christ, may it give pleasure to all who are
honourable.')

24. Engelberg, Stiftsbibliothek, MS Cod. 65
    'ISTA TIBI DONA | GENITRIX ET VIRGO PATRONA //
    FRO[W]INUM   DANTEM | SERVES   APUD
    OMNITONANTEM.' (fol. 1 r)
    ('O Mother and Virgin patroness, protect before God [literally: All-
    Thunderer] Frowin, the giver of these gifts to you.')

25. Engelberg, Stiftsbibliothek, MS Cod. 76
    'Non rodant mures, | non ausint tollere fures, // librum, qui domino |
    datus est a patre Fro[w]ino.' (fol. 1 r)
    ('May mice not gnaw on, may thieves not dare to steal the book that
    was given to the Lord by Father Frowin.')

26. Engelberg, Stiftsbibliothek, MS Cod. 87
    'Ad fratrum lumen | pater hoc Frowine volumen // scribi fecisti, | lux
    luceat o tibi Christi.' (fol. 1 r)
    ('You, Father Frowin, had this book written for the enlightenment of
    the brothers; may Christ's light shine for you [literally: O you!].')

27. Engelberg, Stiftsbibliothek, MS Cod. 88
    'Cur aut unde minus, | habet a mercede Fro[w]inus? // Cum scriptor
    scripsi, | manus autem paruit ipsi.' (fol. [i] v)
    ('Why and for what reason should Frowin have less of the reward [than
    I]? As the scribe I did the writing, but my hand obeyed him.')

28. Engelberg, Stiftsbibliothek, MS Cod. 102[2]
    'Ista tibi dona | genitrix et virgo patrona. // Frowinum dantem |
    serves apud omnitonantem.' (fol. 3 r)
    ('O Mother and Virgin patroness, protect before God [literally: All-
    Thunderer] Frowin, the giver of these gifts to you.')

---

[2] Possibly inserted after Frowin's death; see Steinmann, 'Frowin', 12, n. 21.

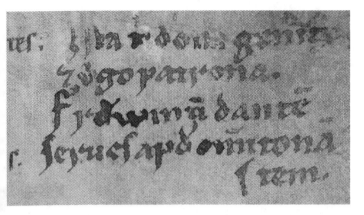

29. Engelberg, Stiftsbibliothek, MS Cod. 139
    'Cernere te Domine | da Frowino sine fine. // Cui mens patrandi |
    fuit hunc librum meditandi.' (fol. 1 r)
    ('O Lord, let Frowin see you without end. For him, pondering this
    book was perfecting the mind.')

30. Engelberg, Stiftsbibliothek, MS Cod. 146
    'Vir bene divinus | abbas aliquando FROWINUS // Me fecit scribi |
    pax sine fine sibi.' (fol. 1 v)
    ('The most religious man and sometime abbot Frowin had me written.
    Peace be with him without end.')

31. Engelberg, Stiftsbibliothek, MS Cod. 1005
    'Contulit ista pie | FROWINUS scripta MARIE.' (fol. 1 r)
    ('Frowin bestowed these writings to the holy [Virgin] Mary.')

32. Engelberg, Stiftsbibliothek, MS Cod. 1007
    'Hunc famulis Christi | librum Frowine dedisti.' (fol. 1 v)
    ('You, Frowin, gave this book to the servants of Christ.')

33. Engelberg, Stiftsbibliothek, MS Cod. 1008
    'Hac de scriptura | Frowine fuit tibi cura. Ut bene credentes | fiant,
    hanc sepe legentes.' (fol. 1 r)
    ('You, Frowin, took care of this writing so that those who read it often
    may become good believers.')

34. Engelberg, Stiftsbibliothek, MS Cod. 1009
    'Contulit ista pie | FROWINUS scripta MARIĘ. // Tu regina poli |
    data munera spernere NOLI.' (fol. 1 r)
    ('Frowin bestowed these writings to the holy Mary. Do not scorn these
    offered gifts, O celestial Queen!')

35. St. Paul in Kärnten, Stiftsbibliothek, MS 30–1
    'FROWIN prelatus | librum fuit hunc operatus.' (fol. 1 r)
    ('Abbot Frowin had this book made.')

36. Milan, Biblioteca Ambrosiana, MS H 51 sup.

    'Sedulitate pia | librum tibi virgo MARIA. // Fecit FROWINUS, reddat ei Dominus.' (fol. 1 r)

    ('Frowin made this book for you, holy Virgin Mary, with pious and painstaking attention; may the Lord repay him!')

© Veneranda Biblioteca Ambrosiana

b) Berchtold (1178–97) [9 colophons]

37. Einsiedeln, Stiftsbibliothek, MS Cod. 240 (641)

    'Vive precor BERHTOLTH, | tibi sit Dominus rogo *fil holth*. // A te quod liber | sim, docet iste liber. // Hunc librum vovi, | nunc promissum tibi solvi. // Ius est, si sapias, | gratus ut accipias.' (p. 1)

38. Engelberg, Stiftsbibliothek, MS Cod. 14

    'Abbas dum fulsit | Berhtolt me scribere iussit, // Unde deus trinus | vere quoque noscitur unus. // Sed mox hic dignus, | castus pater atque benignus // Carnis onus posuit, | praesentia scriptaque linquit // Imperfecta. Sibi | successit munere Christi // Dictus Heinricus; | bonus hic retinereque dignus // Abbatis nomen | perfecit et ipse volumen. // Ergo dei | pia mamma, tui quae filia nati, // Tu genitusque tuus | dignare voluminis huius // Munus blanda datum | bona mitis suscipe gratum.' (fol. 1 r)

39. Engelberg, Stiftsbibliothek, MS Cod. 18
     'Omnis homo hic sancte quamvis studuit fore vite //
          Orci post obitum petiit loca. Gaudia vite //
          Celestis nec promeruit, donec Deus inse //
          Suscipiens hominem celi sic pandere perse //
          Regnum dignatur, dum latroni reseratur //
          Ecce fidem veram lacerando negare probatur //
          Abbas Burchardus nolendo sequi male tardus. //
          Dicit enim, prius in celestia regna beatos //
          Quam Christus natus passusve sit, esse locatos //
          Contra quem Bertholdus abbas noster memorandus //
          Cunctis formula virtutum nobis venerandus //
          Scripsit et obstruxit labra callida falsa loquentis //
          Undique subruit et conclusit eum sapientis //
          Ore, probrans reprobrum cor tetra venena vomentis.' (fol. 123 v)

40. Engelberg, Stiftsbibliothek, MS Cod. 35
     'Hoc pie Christe datum, | Berchtoldi sit tibi gratum.' (fol. 1 v)

41. Engelberg, Stiftsbibliothek, MS Cod. 37
     'Ista tibi dona, | genitrix et virgo patrona // Bertoldum dantem |
     serves apud Omnitonantem.' (fol. 1 r)

42. Engelberg, Stiftsbibliothek, MS Cod. 68
     'Hoc pie Christe datum | Bertoldi sit tibi gratum.' (fol. [i] v)

43. Engelberg, Stiftsbibliothek, MS Cod. 69
     'Hoc pie Christe datum | Bertoldi sit tibi gratum.' (fol. 11 r)

44. Milan, Biblioteca Ambrosiana, MS S 24 sup.
     'Ista tibi dona, | genitrix et virgo patrona // Berchtoldum dantem |
     serves apud Omnitonantem.' (fol. 1 r)

45. Zurich, Zentralbibliothek, MS Rh. 62
     'Istius libri | precepit opuscula scribi // abbas magnificus Domini
     Bertholdus amicus.' (fol. 17 v)

c) Henry I (1197–1223) [2 colophons]

46. Engelberg, Stiftsbibliothek, MS Cod. 67

    'Istud opus danti tibi, | virgo Maria patrona // Heinrico confer sibi |
    tu prece coelica dona.' (fol. 1 v)

    See no. 38.

d) Walter I (1250–67) and/or Walter II (1267–76) [2 colophons]

47. Engelberg, Stiftsbibliothek, MS Cod. 39

    'Hoc opus abbatis | Waltheri sollicitudo. // Cartis aptatis | calamo
    scribe facitudo. // Sub quo collata | Stannes fuit et reputata. //
    Communi mensae | multum non densae.' (fol. 1 r)

48. Engelberg, Stiftsbibliothek, MS Cod. 72

    (a) 'Abbas Waltherus | hoc fecit nempe volumen. // Quo circa
        petimus | capiat coeleste cacumen.' (fol. 1 r)

    (b) 'Sit diz bvoch in felchir frift. / In bvocfhvn . . . vn in tvfchvn ift. /
        Nah monflichir chvnft gefcribin. / Warm were den hindir ftelle
        blibin. / Ein grvoz dim ortfrvm mere. / Dim apt Walthere. /
        Dem wunfche der lefere heilf. / Vñ himilflichif teilf. / Daz felbe
        tvot der verfin schin. / Die da obnan ftant in Latin.' (fol. 72 r)

e) Ulrich I (1296–8) [1 colophon]

49. Engelberg, Stiftsbibliothek, MS Cod. 117

    'Partus virginei sunt anni mille ducenti // Ter denique monas, cum
    scribitur ista studenti // Ulrichis articulis Aurora, sit apta legenti.'
    (fol. 4 v)

f) Rudolph I (1298–1317) [1 colophon]

50. Engelberg, Stiftsbibliothek, MS Cod. 30

    'Hac de scriptura Rudolfe, fuit tibi cura. Fratribus ut fieret, mercesque tibi remaneret.' (fol. 304 r)

g) William (1331–47) [1 colophon]

51. Engelberg, Stiftsbibliothek, MS Cod. 9

    'O vas et noys ens ac numeri decus edens . . . *etc.*') (fol. 129 r)

h) Richene [3 colophons]

52. Engelberg, Stiftsbibliothek, MS Cod. 3

    'Hic currendo bonam | parit, iste loquendo coronam. // Aspera bella gerit | hic, dum sibi praemia quaerit. // Huius scriptura | libri, bona non peritura. // Richene mercatus, | vivet sine fine beatus.' (fol. 281 v)

53. Engelberg, Stiftsbibliothek, MS Cod. 4

    'Littora nauta videns | fit victum post mare ridens, // Sic quia perscripsit | hunc librum Richene risit; // Quare dentur ei, | peto, pax lux et specie.' (fol. 213 r)

54. Engelberg, Stiftsbibliothek, MS Cod. 5 = now Engelberg, Stiftsarchiv, D 126

    'Quod vult dicendo | prudens homo vel faciendo // Aptos aptorum | fines videt officiorum, // Richene magnorum | scribens haec scripta virorum // Institit hoc fine. | Bene quod vivat sine fine // Rerum fons finis | hie ei quod sit dato finis.' (fol. †204 v)

Bibliography

Manuscripts and Archival Sources

Cleveland, Museum of Art
> Purchase from the J. H. Wade Fund 1955.74

Einsiedeln, Stiftsbibliothek
> MS Cod. 166 (413)
> MS Cod. 240 (641)
> MS Cod. 360 (177)

Engelberg,[1]
> Stiftsarchiv
>> A.1
>> B.1
>> B.2

Stiftsbibliothek
> MS Cod. 3
> MS Cod. 4
> MS Cod. 5
> MS Cod. 9
> MS Cod. 12
> MS Cod. 13
> MS Cod. 14
> MS Cod. 15
> MS Cod. 16

---

[1] More than sixty of Engelberg's medieval manuscripts are accessible online in iiiF-compliant format: www.e-codices.unifr.ch/en; those produced under Frowin were digitised in 2011/12 with support from the Stavros Niarchos Foundation: www.e-codices.unifr.ch/en/list/subproject/frowins_library.

MS Cod. 18

MS Cod. 19

MS Cod. 20

MS Cod. 21

MS Cod. 22

MS Cod. 23

MS Cod. 30

MS Cod. 32

MS Cod. 35

MS Cod. 37

MS Cod. 39

MS Cod. 46

MS Cod. 47

MS Cod. 48

MS Cod. 49

MS Cod. 52

MS Cod. 64

MS Cod. 65

MS Cod. 67

MS Cod. 68

MS Cod. 69

MS Cod. 72

MS Cod. 76

MS Cod. 87

MS Cod. 88

MS Cod. 102

MS Cod. 117

MS Cod. 124

MS Cod. 139

MS Cod. 141

MS Cod. 142

MS Cod. 146

MS Cod. 154

MS Cod. 1005

MS Cod. 1007

MS Cod. 1008

MS Cod. 1009

Sarnen, Benediktinerkollegium

MS Cod. membr. 10

St Paul in Kärnten, Stiftsbibliothek

MS 18/1

MS 30–1

Milan, Biblioteca Ambrosiana

MS H 51 sup.

MS S 24 sup.

Vatican, Archivio Apostolico Vaticano, Fondo Bolognetti 332

Zurich, Zentralbibliothek, MS Rh. 62

Edited and Printed Primary Sources

'Annales Engelbergenses, a.1147–1546', in *Annales aevi Suevici* [= *MGH SS* XVII], ed. G. H. Pertz (Hanover: Hahn, 1861), pp. 278–82.

Colophons de manuscrits occidentaux des origines au XVIe siécle, ed. Bénédictins de Bouveret, 6 vols. (Fribourg, CH: Éditions Universitaires, 1965–82).

Delius, P. (ed.), 'Urkundenlese aus dem Lande Unterwalden, ob und nid dem Wald: Von 1148 bis 1512', *Der Geschichtsfreund: Mitteilungen des Historischen Vereins Zentralschweiz*, 14 (1858), 234–69.

Die Tegernseer Briefsammlung des 12. Jahrhunderts, ed. H. Plechl and W. Bergmann (Hanover: Hahn, 2002).

Die Tegernseer Briefsammlung (Froumund), ed. K. Strecker (Berlin: Weidmann, 1925).

Documents Illustrating the Activities of the General and Provincial Chapters of the English Black Monks, 1215–1540, ed. W. A. Pantin, 3 vols. (London: Royal Historical Society, 1931–7).

Frowinus de Monte Angelorum: Explanatio Dominicae orationis. Additus Tractatus de veritate, ed. S. Beck and R. De Kegel (Turnhout: Brepols, 1998).

The Historical Works of Gervase of Canterbury, ed. W. Stubbs, 2 vols. (London: Longman, 1979–80; repr. Cambridge: Cambridge University Press, 2012).

La Régle du Maître, ed./ tr. A. de Vogüé, 3 vols. (Paris: Éditions du Cerf, 1964).

Lehmann, P., P. Ruf, C. E. Ineichen-Eder, et al. (eds.), *Mittelalterliche Bibliothekskataloge Deutschlands und der Schweiz*, 4 vols. (Munich: Beck, 1918–2009).

Letters of Anselm, Archbishop of Canterbury, Vol. 1: The Bec Letters, ed./ tr. S. Niskanen (Oxford: Clarendon, 2019).

Liber ordinis Sancti Victoris Parisiensis, ed. L. Jocqué and L. Milis (Turnhout: Brepols, 1984).

Liber tramitis aevi Odilonis abbatis, ed. P. Dinter (Siegburg: Schmitt, 1980).

'Oratio episcopi vel abbatis ad sanctum sub cuius nomine regit ecclesiam', in *Sancti Anselmi Cantuariensis archiepiscopi opera omnia*, ed. F. S. Schmitt, 6 vols. (Edinburgh: Nelson & Sons, 1938–61), vol. 3, pp. 68–70 (no. 17).

'Ordo Cluniacensis', ed. M. Hergott, in *Vetus disciplina monastica* (Paris: Osmont, 1726; repr. Siegburg: Schmitt, 1999), pp. 136–364.

The Prayers and Meditations of Saint Anselm, tr. B. Ward (New York: Penguin, 1973).

The Rule of St Benedict, ed./ tr. B. L. Venarde (Cambridge, MA: Harvard University Press, 2011).

Sacrorum conciliorum nova et amplissima collectio, ed. G. D. Mansi, 31 vols. (Venice: Zatta, 1758–98).

Vogel, E. G. (ed.), 'Urkunden des Stiftes Engelberg', *Der Geschichtsfreund: Mitteilungen des Historischen Vereins Zentralschweiz*, 49 (1894), 235–62.

Willehelmi Abbatis Constitutiones Hirsaugienses, ed. P. Engelbert and C. Elvert, 2 vols. (Siegburg: Schmitt, 2010).

William of Malmesbury: Gesta regum Anglorum – The History of the English Kings, ed./ tr. R. A. B. Mynors, R. M. Thomson, and M. Winterbottom, 2 vols. (Oxford: Clarendon, 1998–9).

Secondary Literature

'*ababbas, m.*', in *Mittellateinisches Wörterbuch*, ed. O. Prinz and H. Gneuss, 7 vols. (Munich: Beck, 1967–99), vol. 1, p. 5.

Alings, K.-K., '*Auctoritas*: Semantische Studien zu einem Schlüsselbegriff des frühen Mittelalters', unpublished PhD dissertation, University of Cologne, 2019.

Banella, L., 'Boccaccio As Anthologist and the Dawn of Editorial *Auctoritas*', *Mediaevalia*, 39 (2018), 275–97.

Bauer, O., *Frowin von Engelberg (1147–1178)*, '*De laude liberi arbitrii libri septem*': *Versuch einer literatischen und theologiegeschichtlichen Bestimmung der Handschrift 46 von Engelberg* (Louvain: Abbaye du Mont César, 1948).

Bell, N., 'Liturgical Books', in E. Kwakkel and R. M. Thomson (eds.), *The European Book in the Twelfth Century* (Cambridge: Cambridge University Press, 2018), pp. 175–91.

Berndt, G., 'Auctoritas', in *Lexikon des Mittelalters*, Studienausgabe, 9 vols. (Stuttgart: Metzler, 1999), vol. 1, p. 1190.

Bonifazi, R., 'Die beiden Miniaturen der Frowin-Bibel auf Einzelblättern', in C. Eggenberger (ed.), *Die Bilderwelt des Klosters Engelberg: Das*

Skriptorium unter den Äbten Frowin (1143–1178), Bechtold (1178–1197) and Heinrich (1197–1223) (Luzern: Diopter, 1999), pp. 27–30.

Boynton, S., 'The Bible and the Liturgy', in S. Boynton and D. J. Reilly (eds.), *The Practice of the Bible in the Middle Ages: Production, Reception, and Performance in Western Christianity* (New York: Columbia University Press, 2011), pp. 10–33.

Bretscher-Gisiger, C. and R. Gamper (eds.), *Katalog der mittelalterlichen Handschriften der Klöster Muri und Hermetschwil* (Zurich: Graf, 2005).

Brooks C., *Reading Medieval Latin Poetry Aloud: A Practical Guide to Two Thousand Years of Verse* (Cambridge: Cambridge University Press, 2007).

Bruce, S. G., '*Veterum vestigia patrum*: The Greek Patriarchs in the Manuscript Culture of Early Medieval Europe', *Downside Review*, 139 (2021), 6–23.

Bruckner, A. (ed.), *Scriptoria medii aevi Helvetica, Vol. VIII: Schreibschulen der Diözese Konstanz, Stift Engelberg* (Geneva: Roto-Sadag, 1950).

Brügger Buddal, I., and S. Rankovic (eds.), *Modes of Authorship in the Middle Ages* (Toronto: Pontifical Institute of Mediaeval Studies, 2012).

Büchler-Mattmann, H., and G. Heer, 'Die Benediktiner in der Schweiz: Engelberg OW', in E. Gilomen-Schenkel (ed.), *Frühe Klöster, die Benediktiner und Benediktinerinnen in der Schweiz* (Bern: Francke, 1986) [= *Helvetica Sacra* III/1.1]), pp. 595–657.

Chenu, M.-D., 'Auctor, Actor, Autor', *Archivum latinitatis medii aevi*, 3 (1927), 81–6.

Cleaver, L., 'The Monastic Library at Le Bec', in B. Pohl and L. L. Gathagan (eds.), *A Companion to the Abbey of Le Bec in the Central Middle Ages (11th–13th Centuries)* (Leiden: Brill, 2017), pp. 171–205.

Cochelin, I., 'Customaries As Inspirational Sources', in C. Marino Malone and C. Maines (eds.), Consuetudines et Regulae: *Sources for Monastic Life in the Middle Ages and the Early Modern Period* (Turnhout: Brepols, 2014), pp. 27–72.

'Discipline and the Problem of Cluny's Customaries', in S. G. Bruce and S. Vanderputten (eds.), *A Companion to the Abbey of Cluny in the Middle Ages* (Leiden: Brill, 2021), pp. 204–22.

De Hamel, C., *The Posthumous Papers of the Manuscripts Club* (London: Allen Lane, 2022).

De Kegel, R., 'Frowin', in *Historisches Lexikon der Schweiz (HLS)*. https://hls-dhs-dss.ch/de/articles/012646/2006-01-09.

De Vogüé, A., *Community and Abbot in the Rule of Saint Benedict* (Kalamazoo, MI: Cistercian Publications, 1979).

Dengler-Schreiber, K., *Scriptorium und Bibliothek des Klosters Michelsberg in Bamberg* (Graz: Akademische Druck- und Verlagsanstalt, 1979).

Doyle, A. I., 'Publication by Members of the Religious Orders', in J. Griffiths and D. Pearsall (eds.), *Book Production and Publishing in Britain, 1375–1475* (Cambridge: Cambridge University Press, 2007), pp. 109–23.

Duggan, J. T., 'Turoldus, Scribe or Author? Evidence from the Corpus of Chansons de Geste', in Monica L. Wright, N. J. Lacy, and R. T. Pickens (eds.), *'Moult a sans et vallour': Studies in Medieval French Literature in Honor of William W. Kibler* (Amsterdam: Rodopi, 2012), pp. 135–44.

Durrer, R., 'Die Schreiber- und Malerschule von Engelberg', *Anzeiger für Schweizerische Altertumskunde*, 3 (1901), 42–55 and 122–60.

Eales, R., and R. Sharpe (eds.), *Canterbury and the Norman Conquest: Churches, Saints, and Scholars, 1066–1109* (London: Hambledon, 1995).

Eggenberger, C. (ed.), *Die Bilderwelt des Klosters Engelberg: Das Skriptorium unter den Äbten Frowin (1143–1178), Bechtold (1178–1197) and Heinrich (1197–1223)* (Luzern: Diopter, 1999).

Fassler, M. E., 'Hildegard of Bingen and Her Scribes', in J. Bain (ed.), *The Cambridge Companion to Hildegard of Bingen* (Cambridge: Cambridge University Press, 2021), pp. 280–305.

Feiss, H., 'Frowin of Engelberg: His Monastery, His Scriptorium, and His Books', *American Benedictine Review*, 56 (2005), 68–99 and 194–212.

Fisher, M. N., *Scribal Authorship and the Writing of History in Medieval England* (Columbus: Ohio State University Press, 2012).

Garand, M.-C., 'Le scriptorium de Guibert de Nogent', *Scriptorium*, 31 (1977), 3–29.

    Guibert de Nogent et ses secretaires (Turnhout: Brepols, 1995).

Gazeau, V., 'Du *secretarius* au secretaire: Remarques sur un office médiéval méconnu', in L. Jégou, S. Joye, T. Lienhard, et al. (eds.), *Faire lien: Aristocratie, réseaux et échanges compétitifs* (Paris: Publications de la Sorbonne, 2015), pp. 63–72.

Gottwald, B. (ed.), *Catalogus codicum manu scriptorum qui asservantur in Bibliotheca Monasterii O.S.B. Engelbergensis in Helvetia* (Freiburg i. Br.: Typis Herderianis, 1891).

Graumann, T., *The Acts of the Early Church Councils: Production and Character* (Oxford: Oxford University Press, 2021).

Griffiths, J. and D. Pearsall (eds.), *Book Production and Publishing in Britain 1375–1475* (Cambridge: Cambridge University Press, 2007).

Güterbock F., *Engelbergs Gründung und erste Blüte, 1120–1223*, ed. G. Heer (Zurich: Leemann, 1948), pp. 5–31.

Hafner, W., *Der Basiliuskommentar ʒur Regula S. Benedicti: Ein Beitrag ʒur Autorenfrage karolingischer Regelkommentare* (Münster: Aschendorff, 1959).

    'Die Engelberger Bücherfunde', *Librarium*, 6 (1963), 113–18.

    'Die Maler- und Schreiberschule von Engelberg', *Stultifera navis*, 11 (1954), 13–20.

Hamburger, J. F., *The Birth of the Author: Pictorial Prefaces in Glossed Books of the Twelfth Century* (Toronto: Pontifical Institute of Mediaeval Studies, 2021).

Haynes, J., 'Leonine Verse', in C. M. Furey, J. M. LeMon, B. Matz, et al. (eds.), *Encyclopedia of the Bible and Its Reception*, 21 vols. (Berlin: De Gruyter, 2009–23), vol. 16, pp. 128–9.

Hirsch, H., 'Die *Acta Murensia* und die ältesten Urkunden des Klosters Muri', *Mitteilungen des Instituts für Österreichische Geschichtsforschung*, 25 (1904), 209–74.

Hodel, U., and R. De Kegel, 'Engelberg (Kloster)', in *Historisches Lexikon der Schweiẓ (HLS)*. https://hls-dhs-dss.ch/de/articles/008557/2011-03-31.

Hunkeler, L., 'Frowin als Mönch und Abt', in *Der selige Frowin von Engelberg, 1143–1178* (Engelberg: Stiftsdruckerei, 1943), pp. 7–17.

James, M. R., *The Ancient Libraries of Canterbury and Dover* (Cambridge: Cambridge University Press, 1903).

Kaczynski, B. M., 'The Authority of the Fathers: Patristic Texts in Early Medieval Libraries and Scriptoria', *Journal of Medieval Latin*, 16 (2006), 1–27.

'Bede's Commentaries on Luke and Mark and the Formation of a Patristic Canon', in S. Echard and G. R. Wieland (eds.), *Anglo-Latin and Its Heritage: Essays in Honour of A. G. Rigg on His 64th Birthday* (Turnhout: Brepols, 2001), pp. 17–26.

Kennedy, E., 'The Scribe As Editor', in *Mélanges de langue et de littérature du Moyen Age et de la Renaissance offerts à Jean Frappier*, 2 vols. (Paris: Minard, 1970), vol. 1, pp. 523–31.

Kjær, L., *The Medieval Gift and the Classical Tradition: Ideals and the Performance of Generosity in Medieval England, 1100–1300* (Cambridge: Cambridge University Press, 2019).

Könsgen, E., 'Zwei unbekannte Briefe zu den *Gesta regum Anglorum* des Wilhelm von Malmesbury', *Deutsches Archiv für Erforschung des Mittelalters*, 31 (1975), 204–14.

Kujawiński, J., 'Between the Ancient Model and Its Humanistic Revival: The Notion of *Bibliotheca Publica* in the Middle Ages', in M. Delimata-Proch, J. Kujawiński, and A. Krawiec (eds.), Totius mundi philohistor: *Studia Georgio Strẓelczyk octuagenario oblata* (Poznan: Adam Mickiewicz University, 2021), pp. 415–29.

Leemans, J., and B. Meijns, 'Why Are Some Greater than Others? Actors and Factors Shaping the Authority of Persons from Antiquity to the Renaissance', in S. Boodts, J. Leemans, and B. Meijns (eds.), *Shaping Authority: How Did a Person Become an Authority in Antiquity, the Middle Ages and the Renaissance?* (Turnhout: Brepols, 2016), pp. 9–20.

Lehmann, P., 'Das wiedergefundene älteste Bücherverzeichnis des Benediktinerstiftes Engelberg', *Sitzungsberichte der Bayerischen Akademie der Wissenschaften, Philosophisch-Historische Abteilung*, 1964/IV (1964) [= *Beiträge zur mittelalterlichen Bibliotheks- und Überlieferungsgeschichte* I], 5–7.

Mayr-Harting, H., 'Bede's Patristic Thinking As an Historian', in A. Scharer and G. Scheibelreiter (eds.), *Historiographie im frühen Mittelalter* (Vienna: Oldenbourg, 1994), pp. 367–74.

Minnis, A., *Medieval Theory of Authorship: Scholastic Literary Attitudes in the Later Middle Ages*, 2nd ed. (Philadelphia: University of Pennsylvania Press, 2010).

Morin, D. G., 'Trois manuscrits d'Engelberg à l'Ambrosiana', *Revue Bénédictine*, 39 (1927), 297–316.

Muff, G., 'Die Stiftsbibliothek Engelberg: Einhundertundzwanzigtausend Werke – neun davon im Fussboden', *Musik und Liturgie*, 135 (2010), 4–8.

Müller, J.-D., '*Auctor–Actor–Author*: Einige Anmerkungen zum Verständnis vom Autor in lateinischen Schriften des frühen und hohen Mittelalters', in F. P. Ingold and W. Wunderlich (eds.), *Der Autor im Dialog: Beiträge zu Autorität und Autorschaft* (St Gall: UVK, 1995), pp. 17–31.

Müller-Oberhäuser, G. (ed.), *Book Gifts and Cultural Networks from the 14th to the 16th Century* (Münster: Rhema, 2019).

Newton, F. L., *The Scriptorium and Library at Monte Cassino, 1058–1105* (Cambridge: Cambridge University Press, 1999).

Niskanen, S., 'Authorial Publication in the Middle Ages', *Routledge Medieval Encyclopedia Online*, forthcoming.

'From Author to Authority: Anselm's Public Reputation and the Council of Bari (1098)', *Journal of Medieval History*, 49 (2023), 1–22.

'The Emergence of an Authorial Culture: Publishing in Denmark in the Long Twelfth Century', in A. C. Horn (ed.), *The Meaning of Media: Texts and Materiality in Medieval Scandinavia* (Berlin: De Gruyter, 2021), pp. 71–92.

Publication and the Papacy in Late Antiquity and the Middle Ages (Cambridge: Cambridge University Press, 2021).

Norberg, D. L., and J. M. Ziolkowski, *An Introduction to the Study of Medieval Latin Versification* (Washington, DC: Catholic University of America Press, 2004).

Omlin, E., 'Abt Frowin als Gründer der Engelberger Schreiberschule', in *Der selige Frowin von Engelberg, 1143–1178* (Engelberg: Stiftsdruckerei, 1943), pp. 26–35 and 47–53.

Pohl, B., '*Abbas qui et scriptor?* The Handwriting of Robert of Torigni and His Scribal Activity as Abbot of Mont-Saint-Michel (1154–1186)', *Traditio*, 69 (2014), 45–86.

Abbatial Authority and the Writing of History in the Middle Ages (Oxford: Oxford University Press, 2023).

'Who Wrote Paris, BnF, Latin 2342? The Identity of the *Anonymus Beccensis* Revisited', in C. Denoël and F. Siri (eds.), *France et Angleterre: Manuscrits médiévaux entre 700 et 1200* (Turnhout: Brepols, 2020), pp. 153–89.

Pohl, B., and L. Tether, 'Eadmer and His Books: A Case Study of Monastic Self-Publishing', in C. Rozier, S. N. Vaughn, and G. E. M. Gasper (eds.), *Eadmer of Canterbury: Historian, Hagiographer, and Theologian* (Leiden: Brill, forthcoming).

Pollmann, K., 'Christianity and Authority in Late Antiquity: The Transformation of the Concept of *Auctoritas*', in C. Harrison, C. Humfress, and I. Sandwell (eds.), *Being Christian in Late Antiquity: A Festschrift for Gillian Clark* (Oxford: Oxford University Press, 2014), pp. 156–74.

Riddy, F., '"Publication" before Print: The Case of Julian of Norwich', in J. Crick and A. Walsham (eds.), *The Uses of Script and Print, 1300–1700* (Cambridge: Cambridge University Press, 2003), pp. 29–49.

Root, R. K., 'Publication before Printing', *PMLA*, 28 (1913), 417–31.

Rösli, L. and S. Gropper (eds.), *In Search of the Culprit: Aspects of Medieval Authorship* (Berlin: De Gruyter, 2021)

Rouse, R. H., and M. Rouse, *Manuscripts and Their Makers: Commercial Book Producers in Medieval Paris, 1200–1500* (Turnhout: Brepols, 2000).

Salmon, P., *L'abbé dans la tradition monastique: Contribution à l'histoire du caractère perpétuel des supérieurs religieux en Occident* (Paris: Sirey, 1992).

Schleif, C., 'Gifts and Givers That Keep on Giving: Pictured Presentations in Early Medieval Manuscripts', in G. Donavin and A. Obermeier (eds.), *Romance and Rhetoric: Essays in Honour of Dhira B. Mahoney* (Turnhout: Brepols, 2010), pp. 51–74.

Sharpe, R., 'Anselm As Author: Publishing in the Late Eleventh Century', *Journal of Medieval Latin*, 19 (2009), 1–87.

Libraries and Books in Medieval England: The Role of Libraries in a Changing Book Economy. The Lyell Lectures for 2018–19, ed. J. Willoughby (Oxford: Bodleian Library Publishing, 2023).

'The Medieval Librarian', in E. Leedham-Green and T. Webber (eds.), *The Cambridge History of Libraries in Britain and Ireland, Vol. I: To 1640* (Cambridge: Cambridge University Press, 2006), pp. 218–41.

Smith, L., 'Books of Theology and Bible Study', in E. Kwakkel and R. M. Thomson (eds.), *The European Book in the Twelfth Century* (Cambridge: Cambridge University Press, 2018), pp. 192–214.

Steinmann, M., 'Abt Frowin von Engelberg (1143–1178) und seine Handschriften', *Der Geschichtsfreund: Mitteilungen des Historischen Vereins Zentralschweiz*, 146 (1993), 7–36.

'Die Bücher des Abtes Frowin – ein Skriptorium in Engelberg?', *Scriptorium*, 54 (2000), 9–13.

Stöckli, Kuno, 'Codex Engelbergensis 14 und das Engelberger Scriptorium um 1200', *Aachener Kunstblätter*, 47 (1976/77), 15–80.

Sturges, R. S., 'Medieval Authorship and the Polyphonic Text: From Manuscripts Commentary to the Modern Novel', in T. J. Farrell (ed.), *Bakhtin and Medieval Voices* (Gainesville: University Press of Florida, 1996), pp. 122–37.

Tahkokallio, J., *The Anglo-Norman Historical Canon: Publishing and Manuscript Culture* (Cambridge: Cambridge University Press, 2019).

'Rewriting English History for a High-Medieval Republic of Letters: Henry of Huntingdon, William of Malmesbury, and the Renaissance of the Twelfth Century', in E. Winkler and C. Lewis (eds.), *Rewriting History in the Central Middle Ages, 900–1300* (Turnhout: Brepols, 2022), pp. 169–94.

Tether, L., *Publishing the Grail in Medieval and Renaissance France* (Cambridge: D. S. Brewer, 2017).

Thomson, R. M., 'Scribes and Scriptoria', in E. Kwakkel and R. M. Thomson (eds.), *The European Book in the Twelfth Century* (Cambridge: Cambridge University Press, 2018), pp. 68–84.

Von Liebenau, H., *Versuch einer urkundlichen Darstellung des reichsfreien Stiftes Engelberg, St. Benedikten-Ordens in der Schweiz: Zwölftes und dreizehntes Jahrhundert* (Luzern: Räber, 1846).

Von Scarpatetti, B. M. (ed.), *Katalog der datierten Handschriften in der Schweiz in lateinischer Schrift vom Anfang des Mittelalters bis 1550, Vol. II: Die Handschriften der Bibliotheken Bern-Porrentruy* (Zurich: Graf, 1983).

Webber, T., 'Bede's *Historia Ecclesiastica* As a Source of Lections in Pre- and Post-Conquest England', in M. Brett and D. A. Woodman (eds.),

The Long Twelfth-Century View of the Anglo-Saxon Past (Farnham: Ashgate, 2015), pp. 47–74.

'Cantor, Sacrist or Prior? The Provision of Books in Anglo-Norman England', in M. E. Fassler, K. A. M. Bugyis, and A. B. Kraebel (eds.), *Medieval Cantors and Their Craft: Music, Liturgy and the Shaping of History, 800–1500* (Woodbridge: Boydell, 2017), pp. 172–89.

'The Diffusion of Augustine's *Confessions* in England during the Eleventh and Twelfth Centuries', in J. Blair and B. Golding (eds.), *The Cloister and the World: Essays in Honour of Barbara Harvey* (Oxford: Oxford University Press, 1996), pp. 29–45.

'The Libraries of Religious Houses', in E. Kwakkel and R. M. Thomson (eds.), *The European Book in the Twelfth Century* (Cambridge: Cambridge University Press, 2018), pp. 103–21.

'Monastic and Cathedral Book Collections in the Late Eleventh and Twelfth Centuries', in E. Leedham-Green and T. Webber (eds.), *The Cambridge History of Libraries in Britain and Ireland, Vol. I: To 1640* (Cambridge: Cambridge University Press, 2006), pp. 109–25.

'The Patristic Content of English Book Collections in the Eleventh Century: Toward a Continental Perspective', in P. R. Robinson and R. Zim (eds.), *Of the Making of Books: Medieval Manuscripts, Their Scribes and Readers. Essays Presented to M. B. Parkes* (Aldershot: Ashgate, 1997), pp. 191–205.

Zogg, K., 'Maria, Adams Rippe und die verbotene Frucht', in C. Eggenberger (ed.), *Die Bilderwelt des Klosters Engelberg: Das Skriptorium unter den Äbten Frowin (1143–1178), Bechtold (1178–1197) and Heinrich (1197–1223)* (Luzern: Diopter, 1999), pp. 21–6.

Acknowledgements

The research presented in this Element was funded by the award of a Mid-Career Fellowship from the British Academy (2019–21) and supported through a period of research leave at my home institution, the University of Bristol. In discussing and writing up my findings, I have benefitted from the kind help and support of several friends and colleagues whose knowledge of publishing – medieval and modern – far exceeds my own. They are, first and foremost, the members of the now completed project *Medieval Publishing from c.1000–1500* funded by the European Research Commission (2017–22) and hosted at the University of Helsinki, Finland. Samu Niskanen (PI) and his team generously gave me advance access to their project's database and invited me to present work in progress at two of their international conferences, first at Helsinki (2018) and then at Oxford (2022), both of which led to stimulating discussions and intellectual exchanges that have shaped my thinking in important ways. Those whose comments and feedback have had a particularly profound and lasting impact, either directly or indirectly, include Jaakko Tahkokallio, Jesse Keskiaho, Jakub Kujawiński, Lars Boje Mortensen, Jacob Currie, David Ganz, and the two anonymous peer reviewers. Rolf de Kegel (Stiftsarchiv Engelberg), Gregor Jäggi (Stiftsbibliothek Einsiedeln), Petrus Tschreppitsch (Stiftsbibliothek St Paul in Kärnten), and James Kohler (Cleveland Museum of Art) very kindly provided photographic images and/or reproduction permissions. Last but not least, I wish to thank my wife and *auctoritas magnifica* of medieval publishing, Leah Tether, who encouraged me to submit this research for publication as an Element, and who supported me with endless patience and love in seeing it through to completion. It is to her and our daughter Anneli that this Element is dedicated.

Cambridge Elements$^{\equiv}$

Publishing and Book Culture

SERIES EDITOR

Samantha Rayner
University College London

Samantha Rayner is Professor of Publishing and Book Cultures at UCL. She is also Director of UCL's Centre for Publishing, co-Director of the Bloomsbury CHAPTER (Communication History, Authorship, Publishing, Textual Editing and Reading) and co-Chair of the Bookselling Research Network.

ASSOCIATE EDITOR

Leah Tether
University of Bristol

Leah Tether is Professor of Medieval Literature and Publishing at the University of Bristol. With an academic background in medieval French and English literature and a professional background in trade publishing, Leah has combined her expertise and developed an international research profile in book and publishing history from manuscript to digital.

ABOUT THE SERIES

This series aims to fill the demand for easily accessible, quality texts available for teaching and research in the diverse and dynamic fields of Publishing and Book Culture. Rigorously researched and peer-reviewed Elements will be published under themes, or 'Gatherings'. These Elements should be the first check point for researchers or students working on that area of publishing and book trade history and practice: we hope that, situated so logically at Cambridge University Press, where academic publishing in the UK began, it will develop to create an unrivalled space where these histories and practices can be investigated and preserved.

Cambridge Elements ☰

Publishing and Book Culture

Publishing and Book History

Gathering Editor: Andrew Nash

Andrew Nash is Reader in Book History and Director of the London Rare Books School at the Institute of English Studies, University of London. He has written books on Scottish and Victorian Literature, and edited or co-edited numerous volumes including, most recently, *The Cambridge History of the Book in Britain, Volume 7* (Cambridge University Press, 2019).

Gathering Editor: Leah Tether

Leah Tether is Professor of Medieval Literature and Publishing at the University of Bristol. With an academic background in medieval French and English literature and a professional background in trade publishing, Leah has combined her expertise and developed an international research profile in book and publishing history from manuscript to digital.

ELEMENTS IN THE GATHERING

A full series listing is available at: www.cambridge.org/EPBC

Printed in the United States
by Baker & Taylor Publisher Services